MW00791283

Inductive Bible Study Curriculum
Student Guide

OLD TESTAMENT/*Book of*

EXODUS

Set Free, Set Apart

© 2008 Precept Ministries International

Exodus
INDUCTIVE BIBLE STUDY CURRICULUM

© 2008 Precept Ministries International. All rights reserved.
This material is published by and is the sole property of Precept Ministries
International of Chattanooga, Tennessee. No part of this publication may be
reproduced, translated, or transmitted in any form or by any means, electronic or
mechanical, including photocopying, recording, or any information storage and
retrieval system, without permission in writing from the publisher.

Unless otherwise noted, all Scripture quotations are from the New American
Standard Bible, ©1960, 1962, 1963, 1968, 1971, 1972, 1973, 1975, 1977, 1995
by the Lockman Foundation, and are used by permission.

Precept, Precept Ministries International, Precept Ministries International
The Inductive Bible Study People, the Plumb Bob design, Precept Upon Precept,
and In & Out are trademarks of Precept Ministries International.

Enrichment word definitions are taken with permission from
Merriam-Webster, Inc. Merriam-Webster's Collegiate Dictionary. 10th ed.
Springfield, Mass., U.S.A.: Merriam-Webster, 1996, c1993.

ISBN 978-1-934884-17-1

1st edition
Printed in the United States of America

TABLE OF CONTENTS

Exodus

© 2008 Precept Ministries International

© *2008 Precept Ministries International*

1. Inductive Bible Study - _____

2. There are _____ of Inductive Bible Study:

    a. _____ - _____ ?

    b. _____ - _____ ?

    c. _____ - _____ ?

3. Tools of Observation

    a. The _____ questions

b. Mark_____ and_____

c. Make_____

4. Tools of Interpretation

a._____

_____ ! It rules interpretation.

b. _____

c. _____

© 2008 Precept Ministries International

5. Application

    a._____ - resulting in _____

© 2008 Precept Ministries International

God Remembers His Covenant

Do you know what it's like to go from the mountain top to the valley? One minute everything is going your way, then the whole world seems to be against you the next. If this sounds familiar, you can relate to the children of Israel, the descendents of Abraham, Isaac and Jacob.

If you studied Joseph's life, you will remember that his father Jacob moved to Egypt to escape famine in Canaan. And with Joseph as second in command of Egypt, his family prospered. You will see a very different picture in **Exodus**: a new Pharaoh rules, Jacob and Joseph are dead, and their descendents are in a very different position in Egypt... they are enslaved and oppressed.

> "Their cry for help because of their bondage rose up to God. So God heard their groaning; and God remembered His covenant..."
>
> – Exodus 2:23-24

Why? Did they do something wrong? Was God angry with them?

Maybe you are asking the same questions. Perhaps your life, once safe, secure, and loving, changed to one of uncertainty, fear, and difficulty. Maybe your world was turned upside down when your parents divorced or someone in your family became ill or died. Maybe it was when your friends abruptly rejected you. What is life like now? Are you enslaved to anger, unforgiveness, depression, and bitterness? Can anyone deliver you from bondage?

Yes!!! God raised up a man named Moses to **deliver** the children of Israel and He will raise up someone for you as well! Are you ready to learn more? Then study diligently and learn how to be set free!!

ONE ON ONE:

As you open God's Word, remember it is His book, given to you, so that you can know Him and His ways, and love Him with all your heart, mind, body, soul, and spirit by keeping His commandments. Therefore, it's wise to begin each day's study with prayer, asking God to speak to you by His Spirit and through His Word.

Remember, the enemy of your soul doesn't want you to be in the Word. He will try to deter and distract you, but he cannot stop you from persevering.

Also remember that the *good* can be the enemy of the *best*. Busyness with God's work can keep you from God's Word. It's clear from Scripture that God's Word is foundational to what you believe and do. To neglect it is to try to live and work without food, which leads to sickness and death. You cannot neglect God's Word and be spiritually healthy. Look at the Church today to see how true this is.

Commit this unit and each day's study to the Lord. Ask Him for diligence and perseverance to complete the assignments and apply them to your life.

© *2008 Precept Ministries International*

LESSON ONE

1. To really appreciate the book of Exodus and the significance of events in it, start your study by looking at several passages in Genesis.

    > **Cross-references** help you interpret the passage or book you are studying. The Genesis cross-references below will help you understand the children of Israel's history as you observe and interpret the events in Exodus.

    a. Look at God's promise to Abraham, Isaac, and Jacob — the promise of land as an everlasting possession. As you look up each reference, double underline *land* in green and shade it blue. Note what you learn about it. If the text answers any of the 5 Ws and an H (who, what, when, where, why, and how), record it next to the reference.

    b. Using a 3x5 notecard, create a bookmark of key words and symbols you have used already. You will add to the card new key words you discover in the course of the study. *Covenant* should always be on your key word list because everything God does is based on covenant.

    EXAMPLE:

Land

GENESIS 12:1-7

© 2008 Precept Ministries International

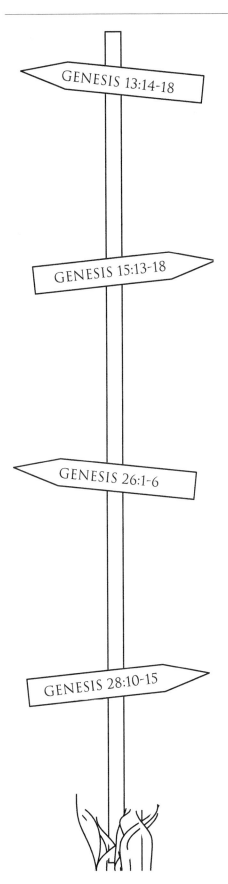

© 2008 Precept Ministries International

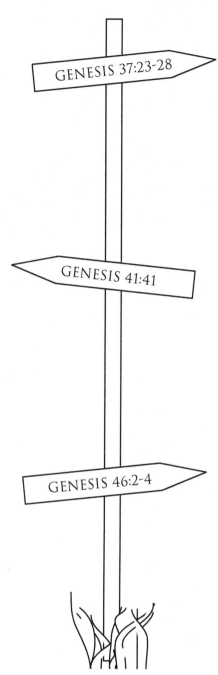

GENESIS 37:23-28

GENESIS 41:41

GENESIS 46:2-4

Joseph is one of Jacob's 12 sons. These next few cross-references will help you learn how Jacob (also called Israel) and his family ended up in Egypt.

2. Read Genesis 50. Mark references to *Egypt* and the *land* promised to Abraham, Isaac, and Jacob. Remember that God changed Jacob's name to "Israel" in Genesis 32:24-28, so both names refer to him. Then briefly record what you learn.

© 2008 Precept Ministries International

© *2008 Precept Ministries International*

LESSON TWO

1.   A map on page 25 will show you the boundaries of the land promised to the descendants of Abraham, Isaac, and Jacob. If God promised Abraham and his descendants this land as an everlasting possession, will it happen?

2. Now read Exodus 1. The book of Exodus is printed out in the Appendix.

   a. As you read this chapter, double underline locations in green. Remember they answer the question "where." These will give you the geographical context of the beginning of Exodus. Also mark time references with a green clock like this: ⏰. You're always asking the 5W and H questions!

   b. Observe "who" are in this chapter. List them and "what" you observe about them on "The Main Characters of Exodus 1" chart at the end of this unit. Record facts that will help you understand them. These facts will tell you *who*, *what*, *when*, *where*, *why*, and *how*. Be sure you record what you learn about the sons of Israel, the king of Egypt who is referred to as "Pharaoh," and the midwives. Then answer the following questions.

     1) How was the Pharaoh in Exodus different from the one in Joseph's time?

     2) What was Pharaoh's problem?

     3) What was his first solution? Did it work? Why or why not?

     4) What was his second solution? Did it work? Why or why not?

     5) What was Pharaoh's third solution?

6) What do you learn from the midwives response to Pharaoh's command? Who do you fear more: God or man?

God knows who fears Him. When you see the word "fear" you may think of things that take your breath away or make your hair stand on end, but it also means a profound reverence and awe. The midwives in Exodus 1 feared God more than Pharaoh and He rewarded them (1:20-21).

           © *2008 Precept Ministries International*

LESSON THREE

Our focus today is Exodus 2: the birth and early years of Moses, a man whose name is repeated throughout God's Word.

1. Read Exodus 2 and mark:

    a. references to *Moses* with a distinctive color or symbol. You don't have to mark Moses throughout Exodus; however it will be useful in this chapter, which introduces him.

    b.   geographical locations and time – important observations.

2. When you finish, record information that answers the 5 W and H questions. When you list your observations, note the chapter and verses they are taken from. In Lesson Four, you will look at some New Testament passages that give you further insight into Moses.

> The <u>5W and H questions</u> help you carefully observe the text. Generally, start with "Who" by listing main characters in the text. Then list "What" you learn about them. You can also list what you learn about the main events by asking, "What is happening? Why is it happening? How? and When?" Make sure you see what is happening in Exodus 2. Be brief in your notes, but diligent in your observations.

3. When you read Exodus 2:24, doesn't it thrill your heart to realize what is behind the words, "and God remembered His covenant with Abraham, Isaac, and Jacob," and to know where in Genesis that covenant was established? Record the cross-reference from Lesson One below that you would use to explain this verse to others.

4. Finally, what does this tell you about God? Record what you learned about Him from this lesson.

> You will learn so much from this awesome book. In God's Word you find pure, unadulterated truth — truth that will equip you for every good work! As you discover more and more about God and His ways, you will find life so much easier to understand and cope with because you will have God's insight and wisdom to guide you.

 © *2008 Precept Ministries International*

LESSON FOUR

Didn't you enjoy the first three lessons and the brief study of Moses' birth and early years! And weren't you thrilled at the way our Sovereign God brings about His purposes! What confidence this should give you, and that confidence will grow with the study of this foundational book.

1. Today, you will read a passage in Acts. If you have time, read what precedes these verses as Stephen, under the inspiration of the Holy Spirit recounts to the Jews a summary of Israel's history before they stone him to death. Record what you learn about Moses from the verses below.

ACTS 7:15-30

2. Now read the following verses and list your observations on Moses. This passage goes beyond the scope of Exodus 2, but it shows how Moses lived.

HEBREWS 11:22-29

© 2008 Precept Ministries International

3. It's always good to reflect on what you read and discuss it with God. Can you apply anything you learned about Moses' example to your life? Any insights into God, knowing He never changes?

   Even if you have only two or three minutes, it's still worth thinking about what you learned. Then, jot down a sentence or two. Use your "Journal on God" in the Appendix to record your insights.

4. Finally, did you gain new insights into Moses' life from these New Testament passages? List them below; this shows how Scripture interprets Scripture. Also, note the references in the margin of your Bible next to the related verses in Exodus.

> Do you realize how much you learned already? And you saw it for yourself! Persevere... you will learn so much about God that will transform your life, that will give you a deeper understanding of why God refers to you as "Beloved" so often in His Word.

© 2008 Precept Ministries International

LESSON FIVE

1. Read Exodus 3:1-4:17. Mark time phrases and locations as in previous lessons. When you mark locations, don't forget to mark *mountain of God;* it's very significant throughout Exodus. Mark it and its synonyms and pronoun in a distinctive way throughout the book and add it to your bookmark.

    Also mark *staff* in chapter 4.

    a. Who are the main characters in this passage?

    b. What is the main subject in Exodus 3:1-4:17?

    c. When does Exodus 3:1–4:17 occur?

    d. Where does it occur?

    e. Why does it occur? What provoked all this? Compare what you saw in Exodus 3 and 4 with Exodus 2:23-25 to answer this question.

    f. Did you notice any key words in this first reading? If so, list them below.

> A **key word** is a word the author uses repeatedly in a significant way, or a word that cannot be removed from the text without leaving it devoid of meaning. A key word can be a noun, descriptive word, or action word that plays a vital part in conveying the author's message.

Having read through Exodus 3:1-4:17, turn your attention to Exodus 3. Did you notice that the conversation between Moses and God doesn't end at Exodus 3:22? Chapters and verses are man-made divisions. However, we will focus on chapter 3 only for the remainder of this unit.

2. Read Exodus 3 again. Mark the following key words: (You may have identified them already!) **affliction** (*suffering, oppression*) with red flames like this: ᴟᴟ and *cry* (*cried*) with a large 𝒞.

    Also look at Exodus 1:11-12 and Exodus 2:23 and mark the same words. While you are in Exodus 2:23, mark **bondage** with a symbol like this: ⌒⌒⌒ (chains and squiggly underline).

    Add these to your bookmark.

3. Pause to reflect on the situation of the Jews. Try to imagine living under those conditions... the slavery and whip of a cruel taskmaster. Maybe you are there — enslaved, but not by a visible taskmaster.

    a. Close today's study by reading the verses below. List what you learn about slavery and freedom.

JOHN 8:31-36

    b. Maybe you believe in God like the Jews mentioned in verse 31. Maybe you acknowledge His Son Jesus Christ. But are you truly His disciple – His student and follower? Are you enslaved and afflicted by persistent, unrelenting sin? Or have you been set free? Think about what John 8:31-36 is teaching, and compare it with the children of Israel in Egypt. Do you need to "cry out" to God because of your slavery and torment? If so, do it now. God put you in this course for a purpose. Write out your responses to these questions below.

© 2008 Precept Ministries International

LESSON SIX

PRECEPT
UPON
PRECEPT®

Exodus
U-1, Lesson 6, Chapter 3

1. Begin today's study by reading Exodus 3 again. Mark Moses' questions in a distinctive color, just the questions, nothing else. Coloring them will help you see them quickly.

2. Now note the questions Moses asks God in Exodus 3:11, 13. Record the questions below and the main points of God's response (don't rewrite the text).

EXODUS 3:11:

Moses' Question –

God's Reponse –

EXODUS 3:13:

Moses' Question –

God's Response –

© 2008 Precept Ministries International

On the day God covenanted with Abraham, He told him that his descendants will be enslaved 400 years, then He will judge the nation they served and bring them out with many possessions.

3. As this unit in the Word comes to a close, stop to reflect on all you learned about God from Exodus 1-3. This will be a real faith builder in your life. Record your thoughts in your "Journal on God."

    As you go through this wonderful exercise, don't rush, but take time to worship God through prayer and praise. Also confess your failings to live according to His Word. To worship God is to acknowledge what He is, to look at His attributes and respond accordingly.

4. Finally, record themes for Exodus 1-3 on the "Exodus At A Glance" chart in the Appendix. Don't labor over them; they should tell you what the chapters are generally about.

> As you finished your first week of study, did you hear His "well done"? You have pleased Him if you have truly listened to what He has to say, if you have given it close attention!

© 2008 Precept Ministries International

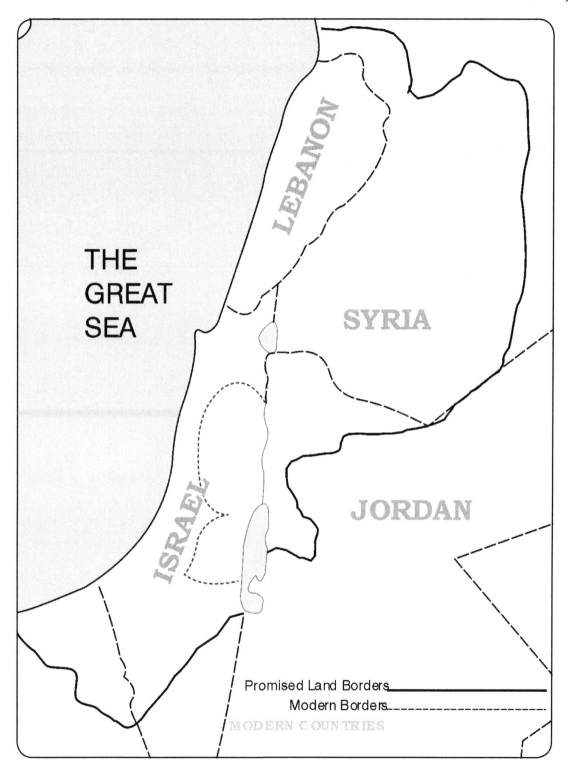

THE
GREAT
SEA

LEBANON

SYRIA

ISRAEL

JORDAN

Promised Land Borders
Modern Borders
MODERN COUNTRIES

© 2008 Precept Ministries International

© 2008 Precept Ministries International

MAIN CHARACTERS OF EXODUS 1

© *2008 Precept Ministries International*

ENRICHMENT WORDS:

Affliction – great suffering.

Bondage – state of being bound under compulsion; captivity.

Deliver – to set free.

Exodus – the second book of the Bible; a mass departure.

© *2008 Precept Ministries International*

Not qualified? Not a problem!

Does God ask us to do the impossible? Yes! But with His help, all things *are* possible.

Apart from God, it's impossible to have joy in a trial, victory over sin, hope in sorrow, wisdom and **discernment** in uncertainty, fulfillment of God's will.

Moses first tried to do things without God but these early attempts to protect and defend his people failed. But when God enabled him, he liberated an entire nation.

What are you trying to do? Did God ask you to do it? Are you walking step by step with God, asking questions, waiting for answers?

Or do you need deliverance…
freedom from fear, hurts and resentments, sin?

In this unit, you will see God unveil His plan for His people and lead Moses to fulfill it. You will see Moses' faith in action – a faith you may relate to. You will see his doubt, hesitation, and shortsightedness. You will see him stepping out, full of reservations, to do God's will and wondering how He will accomplish it. You will see him blinded by his inadequacies, fears, and concerns. These descriptions may deviate from the Bible hero you grew up with, but understanding them can be a faith-builder as you learn that God uses ordinary people to do great things.

© 2008 Precept Ministries International

© *2008 Precept Ministries International*

LESSON ONE

1. This unit will cover Exodus 4 through 7:8 – a rich and exciting time of discovery. Begin today's lesson by reading Exodus 3 and 4 for context. Mark geographical locations and time phrases. By the way, don't forget to commit your study to the Lord in prayer... an awesome thing to do before opening His Book!

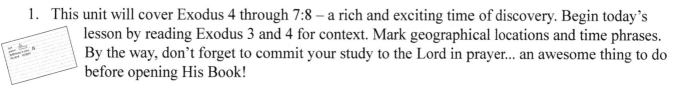

2. Exodus 4 begins where you left off in chapter 3: Moses is still standing barefoot as God talks with him from the burning bush. The chapter begins with Moses asking God a third question. Mark the question in the text with the same color you did in Exodus 3:11 and 13 and record it below.

3. Now read God's response to Moses in Exodus 4:1-9 and mark the key word *sign* with an orange stop sign.

4. What signs, according to Exodus 4, will Moses do to prove that the Lord has appeared to him?

Can you relate to Moses' question? Isn't it similar to what you'd ask God if He told you to deliver a nation from 400 years of oppression? When God grants us opportunities to serve Him, He also supplies our needs to ensure success. By faith we can step out to do whatever He calls us to, trusting His provision.

© 2008 Precept Ministries International

© *2008 Precept Ministries International*

LESSON TWO

1. Has God ever asked you to do something that scared you to death, that you didn't feel qualified for? Do you remember how you responded? What was the outcome? Record some of your story below to help you recall the incident.

2. Now read Exodus 4:1-17. How does Moses respond to God's answer in Exodus 4:2-9? How does God counteract? List the main points in the chart below.

MOSES' OBJECTIONS	GOD'S RESPONSES

   a. Compare Moses' objections with Acts 7:22.

   b. Why do you think he felt inadequate for the task God gave him?

© *2008 Precept Ministries International*

c. Can you see parallels to Moses and others you know, maybe even yourself? Write them out.

3. Look at your observations on God from Exodus 4:1-17 and list your insights below.

4. Think about what you observed in Exodus 3-4 and answer the following:

a. How did God equip Moses and Aaron to lead the children of Israel?

b. Did God give up on Moses when he doubted and hesitated?

© *2008 Precept Ministries International*

---

c. How will this information about God help you when you feel unqualified and incapable of doing what He calls you to do? Remember His name!

"I AM THAT I AM" THE SELF-EXISTENT ONE

Moses looked at himself rather than to the One sending him—I AM. What do you miss when you focus on your circumstances and abilities rather than the Lord? What comfort, peace, victory, truth? He is the Lord of circumstances; He stands outside of them.

"And the heavens are the work of Your hands.
Even they will perish, but You endure;
And all of them will wear out like a garment;
Like clothing You will change them and they will be changed.
But You are the same,
And Your years will not come to an end."
- Psalm 102:26

The phrase "the same" is equivalent to the "I AM" in Exodus 3. Though things in your life change, God never changes. He is and always will be everything you need. No matter the situations or circumstances, God abides forever. He delivers because He's the Savior.

© 2008 Precept Ministries International   37

© *2008 Precept Ministries International*

LESSON THREE

1. Exodus 4:18–5:23 changes scenery. Read this passage and mark key words, geographical locations, and references to time. Add *first-born* to your key word bookmark, and then list what you learn from marking it in Exodus 4.

   As you read, pay attention to where Moses goes, what he takes with him, what happens on the way and when Moses and Aaron arrive at their destination.

2. List main events from this passage.

A CLOSER LOOK AT PHARAOH:

Scholars believe the pharaoh in Exodus is Amenhotep II. The title "**pharaoh**" means "great house," but in 1500 B.C. (around the time of Exodus) it referred to the king himself. Each pharaoh had five names that people weren't permitted to speak so they referred to him by this title only. Pharaohs were absolute monarchs; they ruled armies, courts, and priests of all religions. They defined justice and pronounced their divine authority in daily rituals.

THE MORE YOU KNOW...

3. What does God say to Moses in Exodus 4:21-23? What does this tell you about God and His ways?

4. When you read Exodus 4:24-26, you see circumcision's significance to God. Read Genesis 17:9-14 to learn about this covenant sign. It's a good idea to mark circumcision throughout your Bible. You can draw a symbol of a knife like this ⌣ in red.

    a. Does Genesis 17:9-14 help you understand what happened to Moses on the way to Egypt? What do you see?

    b. What does this action teach you about God? Think about it before you answer; questions like these cause you to stop and reflect on God's character, His ways, and how serious He is. Record your insights in your "Journal on God."

Sometimes we hit a roadblock. It may be sin in our lives that stops us from moving forward. Or God may be reminding us to wait on His timing before He opens the next door. After many objections, Moses moves his family across country to do God's will – a major leap of faith. And now the angel of the Lord tries to kill him... WHAT???

Before God can use Moses to lead His people, God reminds him of the covenant – the same covenant God remembered and is fulfilling through the deliverance of His people. God is the keeper of covenants and His people must live according to them.

          © 2008 Precept Ministries International

LESSON FOUR

1. Read Exodus 6:1-7:7.

    a. Mark key words including *bondage*, geographical locations, and references to time. Note time references in your Bible's margin next to the verse.

    b. Add *listen* to your key word bookmark. Draw an ear like this 𝄌 in green. If the text says *do not listen*, draw a line through your symbol like this: 𝄌.

2. Has Moses resolved his speech problem? Observe the text, carefully noting answers to the 5 Ws and H.

    a. When does this problem occur again?

    b. Why does it resurface? Record what you observe about Moses.

    c. Can you relate to him and his situation? Have difficult circumstances ever caused you to question yourself? To question God?

3. Tomorrow you will look more closely at Exodus 6:1-9; but before you focus on these details, you need to get the big picture. Remember, all Scripture is God-breathed. Men of God spoke and wrote as they were moved by God's Spirit. The Book you are studying is God's Book – inspired, guarded, and kept so you can know God and do great things for Him by His power.

    a. Read Exodus 6:14-27. What are these verses about?

© 2008 Precept Ministries International

b.   On the chart "Moses and Aaron's Family Tree" located at the end of the unit, record Moses and Aaron's genealogy from Levi; also include their sons' names.

c.   Why do you think God records Moses' and Aaron's family tree at this point? Can you think of why He wants to remind them (and us) of their status in their family? (Hint: Do you remember God's promise about *when* Abraham's descendants will return to the Promised Land?)

                                                      © *2008 Precept Ministries International*

LESSON FIVE

Exodus
U-2, Lesson 5, Chapters 6-7

1.   Read Exodus 6:1-9, 28-30, and 7:1-7 and mark the phrase, *I am the Lord*.

2.   What is God's name "YHWH" associated with in this passage? What is God about to do for the children of Israel? List everything in Exodus 6:2-8 that answers this question.

"Lord" (YHWH) is the personal name for God, first used in Genesis 2:4. Jews call it "the Name," "the great and terrible Name," and "the unutterable Name." YHWH (the four-lettered name called the **Tetragrammaton**) is used approximately 7,000 times in the Old Testament. JAH, the shortened form of this name, is the present tense of the verb "to be." Yehovah, Lord, is derived from HAYAH — "to be, to exist."

3.   Now go back to Exodus 3:14-15, which you observed in Unit One. "I AM" means God is the "Self-existent One," complete in and of Himself, eternal, always existing. Isn't that absolutely awesome! Think about it… He is everything and anything you will ever need. It is all found in Him – "from Him, through Him, and to Him are all things," as Romans 11 says. To Him and Him alone belongs all the glory. Compare Exodus 3:14-15 with the following verses.

a. What do you observe about God's name?

b. Read 8:18-24, and 57-59 for context. What do you learn from this passage?

© 2008 Precept Ministries International   43

c. Finally, read John 10:30-33.

   1) Who does Jesus claim to be?

   2) Do people understand His claim? Explain your answer.

   3) Is His claim true? Look up John 1:1-2, 14, and Hebrews 1:1-3, 8 before you answer. Note what these verses teach and record your observations. (Remember what you learned in Isaiah 42:8 and compare it with Hebrews 1:3.)

   4) Why are these claims so important? If Jesus and the Father are not one as He says in John 10:30, and if He did not exist before Abraham as He claims in John 8:57-59, what do these say about Jesus? And if that is the case, can Jesus possibly be Savior of the world? Think about it and record your insights below.

© 2008 Precept Ministries International

5) According to John 8:24, what happens if you don't believe Jesus is "I AM?"

4. Your final assignment today is twofold.

    a. First, record themes for Exodus 4, 5, and 6 on your "Exodus At A Glance" chart.

    b. Then think about what you observed in these three chapters. As you looked at Moses' life, how God dealt with him, and how he weathered these events, did you see any lessons for life? These lessons are often obvious from God's words and actions and people's responses.

        Spend some time reflecting on Exodus 4, 5, and 6. Ask God for lessons for life from these chapters. Record what He shows you below, in the margin of your Observation Worksheets, or in your Bible.

Whatever the trial, whatever the difficulty, all you need to know is what God called you to do. He remains the same; He does not change. When we take our eyes off Him and focus on circumstances, we miss the comfort He gives, the confidence, the sweet, quiet assurance. Look at God in the midst of the storm and have a harbor, a place of refuge in the I AM.

The Lord is my Helper; I will not fear what man will do to me.

© *2008 Precept Ministries International*

MOSES AND AARON'S FAMILY TREE

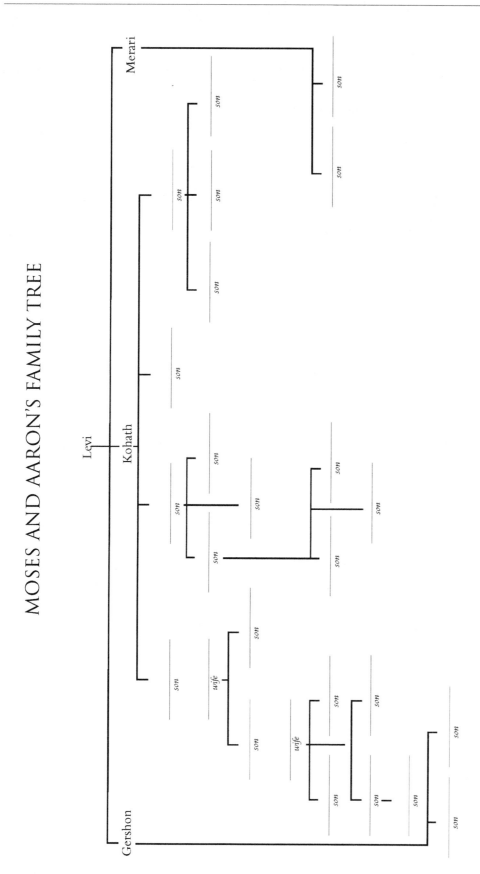

© 2008 Precept Ministries International

© 2008 Precept Ministries International

ENRICHMENT WORDS:

Discernment – the quality of being able to grasp and comprehend what is obscure.

I AM THAT I AM – the Self-Existent One.

Pharaoh – literally "great house;" the title given to kings of Egypt.

Tetragrammaton – the four Hebrew letters usually transliterated YHWH to form the proper name of God, "Yahweh."

© 2008 Precept Ministries International

© 2008 Precept Ministries International

Consequences of a Hard Heart

How many times have you sat in church or school and heard about God? How many stories of His power, love, forgiveness, wrath, righteousness, etc. have you been taught? Have many times have you looked at His will for you in His Word?

> "Yet Pharaoh's heart was hardened, and he did not listen to them, as the Lord had said."
> – Exodus 7:13

Has it changed the way you live? Have you humbled yourself and chosen to believe, repented and started walking in obedience?

Hopefully you have! Or like Pharaoh, have you hardened your heart and refused to obey God?

© 2008 Precept Ministries International

© *2008 Precept Ministries International*

LESSON ONE

Today you will observe Exodus 7-8. Take your time and focus – your only assignment is to observe the text. Watch for details! Ask the 5Ws and H as you read and enjoy the time you spend in God's Word.

1. Read Exodus 7-8, marking the following words and phrases and their synonyms in addition to the key words on your bookmark. Add these to your bookmark.

        a.   *As the Lord commanded, as He commands us, as the Lord had said*

    b. *I am the Lord, that you may know that I am the Lord* (or similar phrases)

    c.   *Pharaoh's heart, harden Pharaoh's heart* (anything about Pharaoh's heart)

    d.   *Let My people go that they might serve Me*

    e.   *Wise men, sorcerers, magicians of Egypt*

    f.   Don't forget to mark references to time and geographical locations.

© 2008 Precept Ministries International

© *2008 Precept Ministries International*

LESSON TWO

1. Read Exodus 7-8 again. As you read about each plague, record the pertinent information on the "God's Plagues on Egypt" chart at the end of this unit. Record the plagues in the order they occur in the text and then fill in the other columns when appropriate.

2. Record themes for Exodus 7 and 8 on the "Exodus At A Glance" chart.

> A <u>chapter theme</u> is a summary statement for the chapter. After you complete your observations, determine the main point(s) and write a brief statement that will help you remember the chapter's contents. When you complete your study of Exodus, you will have your own table of contents.

3. Answer the following questions to help you understand the events in these chapters and those to follow.

   a. What does God say He will do to Pharaoh in Exodus 7:3? Why?

   b. How will God bring His people out?

   c. Look at Genesis 15:13-14 once more. What do you see that helps you understand Exodus 7:4? What does this tell you about God?

   d. What will the Egyptians know when God brings these judgments on them?

   e. How do Moses and Aaron respond to God's command?

4. Although you already recorded this on your chart, it is important to make sure you understand what is happening – how did Pharaoh respond to Aaron's staff turning into a serpent and the Nile turning to blood? Record your answer as it appears in the text.

5. What did Pharaoh ask Moses to do about the frogs? Do you think Pharaoh finally had a change of heart? How do you know?

6. Go back and look at every place you marked *magicians*. What did you learn about them? How does their power compare to God's?

7. Where did the swarms of flies *not* go in Egypt? Why?

8. What did Pharaoh tell Moses to do about the flies? How did God respond? How did Pharaoh?

9. Write down at least three things you learned about God from these chapters and how you can apply them to your life in your "Journal on God."

> Isn't it amazing that God told Abraham more than 400 years prior to these events that his descendents will be enslaved and oppressed and that He will judge the nation they served. Moses, Aaron the Hebrew people and the Egyptians were watching prophecy unfold right before their eyes! They were seeing the one, true God make Himself known. Moses and Aaron saw and obeyed; Pharaoh saw and hardened his heart. Who are you more like?

© *2008 Precept Ministries International*

LESSON THREE

1. Read Exodus 9 and 10. Mark references to *sin* in brown along with the other key words on your bookmark.

2. Record your insights on the plagues in the appropriate columns.

3. Record themes for Exodus 9 and 10 on the "Exodus At A Glance" chart.

© 2008 Precept Ministries International

© *2008 Precept Ministries International*

LESSON FOUR

1. Answer the following questions to help you interpret Exodus 9.

    a. What does God say to Pharaoh at the beginning of chapter 9?

    > Did you notice you're answering 5W and H questions? Train yourself to ask these as you observe Scripture. They will help you to become a better student of the Word.

    b. Look back at chapters 7 and 8. How many times has He said this to him?

    c. Does this tell you anything about God? What? Look at Psalm 103:8 and record what you learn about God.

    d. What did the magicians do after the plague of boils came? What does this tell you about their power?

    e. God says He could have sent a pestilence to cut Pharaoh and the Egyptians off from the earth. Why didn't He?

    f. Where did hail *not* fall? Why? Look back at 8:22-23 if you don't remember.

g. What is Pharaoh's response to the plague of hail? Does Moses believe Pharaoh's heart changed? How do you know?

h. Was Moses right about Pharaoh? Explain.

2. Now, answer the following questions to better understand Exodus 10.

a. What does God say He has done to Pharaoh at the beginning of this chapter?

b. Based on your observations of Pharaoh, was God unjust? Why or why not?

c. God reveals Pharaoh's problem in verse 3. According to this verse, what is a hard heart?

d. How does Pharaoh respond to the plague of locusts? Was he sincere? How do you know?

e. What does Pharaoh threaten Moese with after the plague of darkness? Was Moses afraid? Why do you think Moses responded as he did?

© *2008 Precept Ministries International*

3. Now, think about what you learned from these two chapters. Write down at least three things you learned about God in your "Journal on God" and three things you learned from Pharaoh's example in the space below.

© *2008 Precept Ministries International*

Note: You will need two days to complete these lessons. Complete as much as you can the first day and finish the rest on the second day.

What is a hard heart? Why did God harden Pharaoh's heart? Does He do this to others? Does this mean He doesn't give people the chance to repent and turn to Him?

You probably asked these questions as you worked through the lessons in this unit. As you continue to study Exodus and other scriptures, you will discover that Pharaoh was not the only person to harden his heart and have his heart hardened by God. It's important for you to examine this topic closely to understand God's actions so you will not harden your heart.

Today you will look at several passages that deal with hard hearts. Ask the Holy Spirit to give you understanding before you begin.

> "But the Helper, the Holy Spirit, whom the Father will send in My name, He will teach you all things, and bring to your remembrance all that I said to you."
>
> —John 14:26

1. You may need to review previous lessons to answer the following questions about Pharaoh.

    a. What opportunities did Pharaoh have to know God and His power?

    b. Did Pharaoh know what God required of him? What was it?

    c. How does God describe Pharaoh's hard heart? (Exodus 10:3)

2. Now, look at another example of when God hardened people's hearts. Read the verse in the sign post and answer the following questions. (Read verses 16-20 to help you understand the context.)

   a. Why did God harden their hearts?

   b. The land Joshua and the Israelites are conquering is the land God promised to Abraham. Genesis 15:6 explains why Abraham's descendants will not posses the land until the fourth generation, when they return from the land where they will be enslaved and oppressed 400 years (you know that land is Egypt from your study of Exodus).

      According to Genesis 15:6, why does God wait to give Abraham and his descendants the land? How long will they wait?

   c. Do you remember what God told Pharaoh in Exodus 9:16? Read it again and write out why God allowed Pharaoh and his people to remain. Do you think "all the earth" includes the peoples Joshua fought in the land 40-50 years following the exodus?

   d. Does this information help you understand why God hardened their hearts? Record your insights below.

3. Does God only harden pagans' hearts – like the Egyptians and those living in Canaan?

   a. Read the verse in the sign post on the next page and answer the following questions.

    © *2008 Precept Ministries International*

1) Who did God judge for having hard hearts?

2) How long did they witness God's works in the wilderness? (Remember these are the same people Moses led out of Egypt – what other miracles did they see?)

3) What does God say the root of their problem was?

4) What consequences did they face for their hardness?

b. Read the following verses – Paul's address to the men of Ephesus.

1) What is Paul teaching about? How long does he stay in Ephesus?

2) How do some of those listening respond?

3) What does Paul do as a result?

© 2008 Precept Ministries International

Because of their hard hearts, the children of Israel in the wilderness were not allowed to enter the Lord's rest. Paul reasoned with the Jews at Ephesus then withdrew from them when some became hardened and disobedient. These are high prices to pay!

Righteous – just, lawful, be in the right, morally right, or justifiable.

Judge – to govern, vindicate, punish.

Equity – evenness, uprightness, straightness, freedom from bias or favoritism.

4. Read the following verses and record what you learn about God as the judge of all mankind.

PSALM 7:9-11

PSALM 9:7-8

PSALM 51:4

PSALM 75:1-8

This is from David's prayer of repentance after he committed adultery with Bathsheeba and murdered her husband.

© 2008 Precept Ministries International

a. Is God right when He judges? Why?

b. Do these verses help you understand why God hardens people's hearts?

5. Even if you don't fully understand, can you still believe God is good, righteous, and equitable when He judges? Job questioned God's judgment. Look at these excerpts from God's responses to him and write down what you learn.

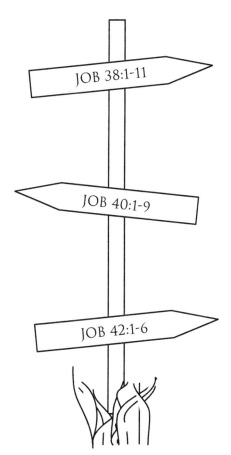

JOB 38:1-11

JOB 40:1-9

JOB 42:1-6

© 2008 Precept Ministries International

6. Whew! That's a lot! One final assignment before you finish this lesson. Its important because you need to know how to apply what you learned… otherwise you have wasted your time!

How can you keep from having a hard heart? Explain in your own words from these passages and from what you have seen in this lesson.

HEBREWS 3:12-15

JOHN 12:36-41

You have worked hard and learned a lot! God reveals Himself in Scripture, but what do you do when you still don't understand something about Him or what He does? Ultimately you must decide if you believe what Isaiah 55:8-9 says, "For My thoughts are not your thoughts, nor are your ways My ways,' declares the Lord. 'For as the heavens are higher than the earth, so are My ways higher than your ways and My thoughts than your thoughts.'"

God gave Pharaoh many opportunities to know Him and humble himself and each time Pharaoh hardened his heart. Pharaoh made his choice and then God hardened his heart to then demonstrate His power to the whole earth. Will you be like Pharaoh? Will you harden you heart or will you humble yourself? Will you believe what you have seen and heard about the Lord and obey?

© 2008 Precept Ministries International

GOD'S PLAGUES ON EGYPT

THE PLAGUES	PHARAOH & EGYPTIANS' RESPONSE	IMPACT ON HEBREWS

© *2008 Precept Ministries International*

ENRICHMENT WORDS:

Equity – evenness, uprightness, straightness, freedom from bias or favoritism.

Judge – to govern, vindicate, punish.

Righteous – just, lawful, be in the right, morally right, or justifiable.

Exodus

© 2008 Precept Ministries International

UNIT FOUR

The Passover Lamb

What does it take to make us realize that God means what He says... that He is God and cares for His people?

You are about to look at one of the most amazing events detailed in the Bible – God's miraculous deliverance of His people. You've studied the events leading up to Israel's release and looked at the consequences of a hard heart. Sin and disbelief cost Egypt a lot. Now Pharaoh's pride will cost him what is most dear to him.

Isn't this a picture of many people today? Too hard hearted and full of pride to submit to God! What about you? What price are you willing to pay for today's gratification, for a momentary pleasure?

What's most amazing about the account you'll study in this unit is God's provision through the Passover. This event's significance touches every child of God... you'll gain new perspective on the Father's great love for the world... His sacrifice... His plan before the foundation of the world.

Exodus
U-4, Chapters 11-13

© 2008 Precept Ministries International

LESSON ONE

You are about to study one of the most important events in Scripture, an event that casts an eternal shadow down through the ages, an event whose substance man can accept with eternal benefits or ignore with eternal consequences.

1. Read Exodus 10:21-11:10 to put yourself into context. Then mark your Exodus 11 Observation Worksheet, watching for key words you have marked previously. Don't forget to mark each occurrence of *first-born* – it's especially important in this passage. As you observe the text, note where Moses is and where he goes.

2. When you finish, list your observations on the chart below. Answer the 5Ws and H about each.

MOSES	GOD'S PEOPLE	PHARAOH	THE EGYPTIANS

© 2008 Precept Ministries International

3. Record what you learned about God, His character and ways, from Exodus 11 in the "Journal on God."

4. Record a theme for Exodus 11 on your "Exodus At A Glance" chart.

> Recording what you learn about God will help you develop a biblical understanding of Him that will lay an unshakable foundation – one that can withstand the earthquakes of life. If you really know God, your faith won't collapse; you won't find yourself buried in the rubble of life's calamities and trials.
>
> As you study, talk to God about what you have learned about Him and how it pertains to your relationship with Him.

© 2008 Precept Ministries International

LESSON TWO

Exodus 12 is full of riches to mine by careful observation.

1. Today, read chapter 12 to get an overview before you mark the text.

2. Now re-read chapter 12 and mark the following new key words. Remember to mark pronouns so you won't miss anything. Also mark words from your key word bookmark.

        a.   *lamb*

    b.   *Passover (pass over you)*

    c. *leaven*

    d. *unleavened*

    e. *blood*

    f. *circumcised*

© 2008 Precept Ministries International

© *2008 Precept Ministries International*

LESSON THREE

1. Review Exodus 12 and list everything you learn about the **Passover** and the Feast of Unleavened Bread on the chart at the end of this unit. It's important to get these details down so you will have a thorough biblical understanding of the Passover.

> Ask 5W and H questions. When you find answers, put them on your list. Listing will help you focus on topics and see details clearly.

2. The New Testament says "Christ our Passover also has been sacrificed." Read the following passage and mark *Passover* and *leaven*. These verses show that the Jewish Passover foreshadows believers' redemption from Satan's kingdom and power — how incredible! This event, which occurred thousands of years ago became a picture of salvation! Think about this as you do this assignment. Think... and be blessed! Write out your response to this insight below.

1 CORINTHIANS 5:7-8

3. Record a theme for chapter 12 on your "Exodus At A Glance" chart.

© *2008 Precept Ministries International*

LESSON FOUR

Your observations of Exodus 13 will be foundational to understanding other portions of the Word and will help you realize Exodus' importance. Like Genesis, Exodus provides a picture of man's redemption and worship of God.

1. Read Exodus 13, observing and marking it carefully using your key word bookmark.

2. Add new insights on the *Passover* to your chart at the end of this unit.

3. Record a theme for chapter 13 on the "Exodus At A Glance" chart.

© 2008 Precept Ministries International

LESSON FIVE

Exodus
U-4, Lesson 5, Chapter 13

1. *First-born* is a key word throughout your study. Starting with Exodus 4:22 through Exodus 13, list your observations from marking **first-born** if they answer *who, what, when, where, why,* or *how*.

> The Hebrew word for "first-born" is "bekor." "First-born" not only means first-born from the womb, but it can also denote preeminence and associated responsibilities, rights, and privileges.

It's interesting that God commanded Moses to tell Pharaoh that Israel was His son, His first-born (Exodus 4:22). Pharaoh believed he alone was "the son of the gods." God told Pharaoh from the beginning the consequences of refusing to let His first-born go: He will kill Pharaoh's first-born.

2. Look up the following cross-references on *first-born*. Examine each one asking the 5Ws and H, and record what you learn.

EXODUS 34:18-20

© 2008 Precept Ministries International

83

U-4, Lesson 5, Chapter 13

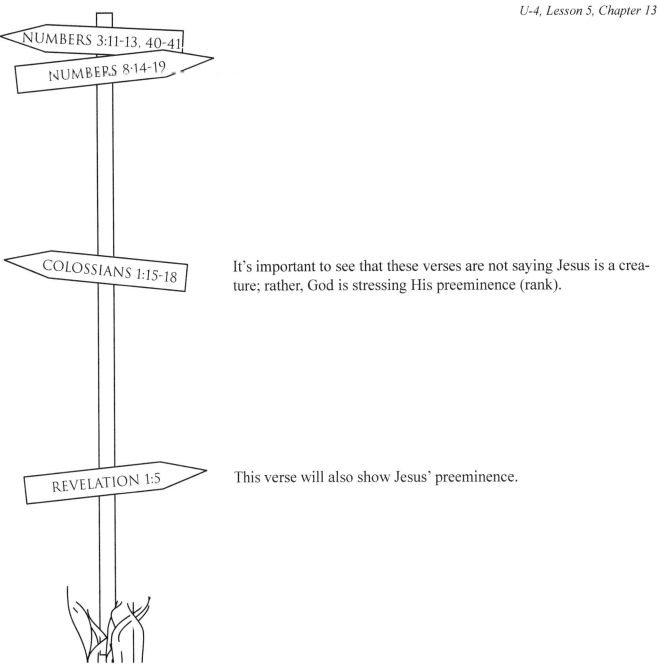

It's important to see that these verses are not saying Jesus is a creature; rather, God is stressing His preeminence (rank).

This verse will also show Jesus' preeminence.

© 2008 Precept Ministries International

3. Summarizing facts you gathered in your own words can seal the understanding of a truth in your mind. Either in list form or paragraph style, summarize what you learned from looking at *first-born*.

4. You're doing great! Before you finish this unit look at one more thing. Did you notice that Exodus 12:38 mentions a mixed multitude who left Egypt with the sons of Israel? Compare this with Numbers 11:1-6 and 1 Corinthians 10:1-12 and answer the following:

   a. How did this "rabble" influence Israel? How is Israel described?

   b. What can you apply to your life from these passages? What influences you?

© 2008 Precept Ministries International

Did you realize that understanding the Old Testament helps you understand more about Jesus? God commanded Israel to set apart every first-born male among them as a reminder of what God did for them in Egypt. We now know that this was also a picture of Jesus Christ. Although you may not understand every aspect of this concept you can thank God for what you have learned.

© 2008 Precept Ministries International

THE INSTITUTION OF THE FIRST TWO JEWISH FEASTS

PASSOVER	FEAST OF UNLEAVENED BREAD

© 2008 Precept Ministries International

THE INSTITUTION OF THE FIRST TWO JEWISH FEASTS

PASSOVER	FEAST OF UNLEAVENED BREAD

© 2008 Precept Ministries International

ENRICHMENT WORDS:

First-born – first child in birth order; also denotes preeminence and associated responsibilities, rights, and privileges.

Passover – the exemption of the Israelites from the slaughter of the firstborn in Egyptian; a Jewish holiday beginning on the 14th of Nisan and commemorating the Hebrews' liberation from slavery in Egypt.

© 2008 Precept Ministries International

UNIT FIVE

Trust in Trials

Are you between a rock and a hard place? Do you feel like your back is against a wall with a barrier standing before you? Does no solution, escape, or relief seem to be in sight?

Maybe you've suffered and stressed in these circumstances for some time. How have you responded? Have you questioned God? Have you complained? Have you been angry with Him for bringing these difficulties into your life?

In every trial, God promises He won't allow more than you can bear without a way of escape. He knows where you are and has a purpose in it all. You simply have to trust Him. One thing is certain… you have faced trials in the past, you are in one now, or you will be soon. How will you cope? How will you prepare? Do you know what God has to say to you in the midst of your battle?

PRAYER

ONE ON ONE:

Do you realize you are studying *His* account of history – *His* story, recorded by men *He* has inspired? What insight, what assurance, what confidence it can bring into your life! As you begin this unit, pause for a few minutes to thank God for this privilege; tell Him you want to handle it in a responsible way. Ask Him for insight and understanding, and tell Him you want to walk in a manner worthy of Him.

© *2008 Precept Ministries International*

LESSON ONE

1. Begin today's lesson by reading Exodus 13:17-14:31 to understand the context of the exodus from Egypt. As you read, mark geographical locations and then consult the Exodus map located in the Appendix. Trace the journey of God's first-born; you'll see that He did not lead them through the Philistines' land.

2. Now read the same passage again, marking key words and phrases. Mark references to the *pillar of cloud*, *pillar of fire*, and time phrases.

© 2008 Precept Ministries International

© *2008 Precept Ministries International*

LESSON TWO

1. Today you will focus on the details of the children of Israel's exit from Egypt through an exercise called storyboarding. When a commercial or movie is made, the scenes are laid out on a "storyboard." A box is drawn for each scene to be shot and the scene is sketched within the box. This helps producers visualize what they want to capture on film.

   You will notice a series of boxes at the end of this unit – your storyboard for Exodus 13:17-14:31. Complete the following for each scene:

   a. Record the location of the event on the line below the box.

   b. Draw stick figures or a cartoon-type scene of what happens in those particular verses. You can even draw little clouds over the speakers and write in a few words to convey their points.

   c. Finally, look for references to the Lord that are followed by action verbs (things He's doing) and record them on lines under the appropriate storyboard box.

> Did storyboarding help you visualize these events? Did it make you appreciate the powerful way God guided and defended His people? When the children of Israel saw a dead-end, God showed them a way of escape. When the enemy camped beside them, the Lord was their shield. When they were nearly overcome, God defeated the Egyptians. Just think... He is the same God today who can move on your behalf. Trust Him... Believe in Him.

© *2008 Precept Ministries International*

1. Read Exodus 15.

    a. Carefully observe and mark the chapter using your key word bookmark.

    b.   You will be introduced to a new person in this chapter. This is the first time her name appears in the Bible, so list in the margin what the text tells you about her.

    c. Also note geographical locations and indicators of time. Trace the people's journey on your map.[1]

2. Fill out the chart at the end of the lesson. Observe the song of praise and list what you learn about the Lord (including why He did the things He did), the children of Israel, and those He came against.

JEHOVAH
RAPHA
"I, THE LORD,
AM YOUR HEALER."

3. Look at the contrast between what God did *for* the **redeemed** and what He did *to* His enemies. What can you apply to your life from these insights?

4. Now, look at the list on the Lord. What do you see about God that will change how you view the next trial you encounter? Record your thoughts in your "Journal on God."

5. Write out below the problem the people faced in 5:22-27 and God's solution.

---

[1]Opinions differ on the location of some sites.

© 2008 Precept Ministries International

a. What do you think about their response in light of what God did for them in Egypt and at the Red Sea?

b. How quickly do you forget about God's faithfulness and provision? What can you apply to your life from these verses?

6. Record themes for Exodus 14 and 15 on your "Exodus At A Glance" chart.

How does all this affect your understanding of God? Do you want to love and trust Him more? Are you awed by Him or skeptical of these "fantastic stories?" Remember, this study's purpose is not merely to teach you Exodus but also to help you know the God behind the exodus.

Persevere; give it all you have. Nothing will build your faith more than studying God's Word and then living in light of the truth.

© 2008 Precept Ministries International

THE LORD	CHILDREN OF ISRAEL	THOSE HE CAME AGAINST

© 2008 Precept Ministries International

© 2008 Precept Ministries International

LESSON FOUR

1. Observe Exodus 16, asking the 5Ws and H. Mark key words from your bookmark along with the following (including synonyms and pronouns):

   a. *test* (Mark it in Exodus 15:25 also.)

   b. **grumble**, *grumblings*, *grumbled* (Mark it in Exodus 15:24 also.)

   c. *seventh day* and *sabbath* (Although God sets apart the seventh day in Genesis 2:1-3, this is the first time the Bible uses the word "**sabbath**.")

   d. *manna* and *bread*.

   2. Record a theme for Exodus 16 on your "Exodus At A Glance" chart.

© 2008 Precept Ministries International

Exodus
U-5, Lesson 4, Chapter 16

© 2008 Precept Ministries International

1. What did God say and do so people would know He is the Lord, YHWH? And who did He want to know this? Look back through your Exodus 7-16 Observation Worksheets and list everything you learned from marking *know that I am the Lord*. This assignment will not only strengthen your faith but also help seal these things in your memory so the Holy Spirit can bring them to mind when you need them.

> Marking key words and phrases makes it easy to find all the information in a chapter or book to create a list.

2. Yesterday you marked references to *manna* (*bread*).

    a. Look up the following cross-references and record what you learn about it:

DEUTERONOMY 8:1-3

JOSHUA 5:9-12

MATTHEW 4:4

JOHN 6:30-35

JOHN 6:47-58

© 2008 Precept Ministries International

b. Now, evaluate what you've learned about manna from these passages and Exodus 16 by answering the 5Ws and H. For example, who gave the manna, who ate it, what is it, what did it symbolize? etc. Simply go through the 5Ws and H one at a time and answer all you can. Make sure your answers are from the Bible and you will be on secure ground!

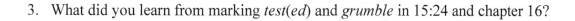

3. What did you learn from marking *test(ed)* and *grumble* in 15:24 and chapter 16?

   a. How did the children of Israel respond to God's testing?

   b. Who do Moses and Aaron say the children of Israel are grumbling against?

   c. How soon after the Red Sea deliverance did they begin to grumble? What did they forget about the Lord?

d. Do you complain when things are uncertain… in times of testing? What can you learn from the children of Israel's response to God? Spend time evaluating your response to difficult circumstances. What is God teaching you?

4. Look up the following verse and list what you learn.

PHILIPPIANS 2:14-16

Well done! God will honor the time you've committed to studying His Word. You still have a lot to cover, but the truths you've learned will sustain you for life if you will cling to them and live by them.

The children of Israel saw God's power demonstrated in Egypt in ways we will never see, but three days following their deliverance at the Red Sea, their faith began to fade. Does this convict if you've allowed doubt and fear to overshadow His miraculous hand in your life? He is your healer, provider, and warrior, and will lead you where He wants you to be. Even if you are in the "wilderness" right now, if you are living in His will, you are exactly where you need to be.

Hebrews 11:6 says "without faith it is impossible to please Him." So run with **endurance** so that you may receive the reward of the faithful.

© 2008 Precept Ministries International

SCENES FROM EXODUS 13:17-22

Exodus
U-5, Chapters 14-16

EXODUS 13:17-18

EXODUS 13:19

LOCATION

LOCATION

WHAT GOD DID

WHAT GOD DID

EXODUS 13:20

EXODUS 13:21-22

LOCATION

LOCATION

WHAT GOD DID

WHAT GOD DID

© 2008 Precept Ministries International

SCENES FROM EXODUS 14

EXODUS 14:1-4

LOCATION

WHAT GOD DID

EXODUS 14:5

LOCATION

WHAT GOD DID

EXODUS 14:6-9

LOCATION

WHAT GOD DID

EXODUS 14:10-12

LOCATION

WHAT GOD DID

EXODUS 14:13-14

LOCATION

WHAT GOD DID

EXODUS 14:15-18

LOCATION

WHAT GOD DID

© 2008 Precept Ministries International

SCENES FROM EXODUS 14

EXODUS 14:19-20

LOCATION

WHAT GOD DID

EXODUS 14:21-25

LOCATION

WHAT GOD DID

EXODUS 14:26-30

LOCATION

WHAT GOD DID

EXODUS 14:31

LOCATION

WHAT GOD DID

© 2008 Precept Ministries International

© 2008 Precept Ministries International

ENRICHMENT WORDS:

Endurance – ability to withstand hardship or adversity; especially the ability to sustain a prolonged stressful effort or activity.

Grumble – mutter in discontent.

Jehovah Rapha – the Lord who heals.

Persevere – persist in a state, enterprise, or undertaking in spite of opposition and/or discouragement.

Sabbath – literally to cease, desist; weekly day of rest and abstention from work imposed on the Israelites.[1]

---

[1] Achtemeier, Paul J., Publishers Harper & Row, and Society of Biblical Literature. *Harper's Bible Dictionary*. 1st ed. San Francisco: Harper & Row, 1985, p. 888.

© *2008 Precept Ministries International*

Passing the Test

How do you react to disappointment? Perhaps you didn't make the team, your friends turned against you, your family is falling apart, life isn't what you expected. Where do you turn at these low points?

If you have ever struggled to trust God, you're not alone. But God's Word offers countless examples of His faithfulness that will grow your faith to trust Him in hardships. And sincere faith in God will sustain you through life's toughest blows and send a loud message to a watching world.

> "Moses said to them, 'Why do you quarrel with me? Why do you test the Lord?'"
>
> – Exodus 17:2

As you delve into this next portion of Exodus, watch God's faithfulness to His people in their times of testing. Look also for the marks of godly leadership. Together, these lessons for life can equip you to be a godly example despite disappointment, temptation, or sorrow.

© 2008 Precept Ministries International

© *2008 Precept Ministries International*

LESSON ONE

1. You will study only two chapters in this unit, but they are powerful — rich with practical application, especially chapter 17! After prayer, read Exodus 17.

   a. Mark geographical locations and note where the chapter divides.

   b. Fill in the blanks below with the verses that comprise each segment division, then record the main event in each one.

      1) Exodus 17: 1 - _____

      2) Exodus 17: _____ - _____

2. Now locate where the events take place on the "Israel's Journey" map in the Appendix.

3. Read Exodus 17:1-7 and mark key words including *quarrel*. Don't forget to mark references to *testing*.

4. Why do you think Moses called the people's desire for water a "test?" Think about all God provided for them up to this point and write out your thoughts.

Exodus
U-6, Lesson 1, Chapter 17

How many times has God provided for you? How many blessings has He given you? Do you still doubt Him? Do you fall to pieces or get angry at God when your circumstances are difficult? If you have ever doubted, complained, or quarreled with God about your circumstances it may be because you don't trust Him.

How can you change? How can you trust Him regardless of your circumstances? You need faith! "Now faith is the assurance of things hoped for, the conviction of things not seen. For by it the men of old gained approval. By faith we understand that the worlds were prepared by the word of God, so that what is seen was not made out of things which are visible" (Hebrews 11:1-3).

How do you grow in your faith? You are doing it right now because "faith comes from hearing, and hearing by the word of Christ." (Romans 10:17) Keep studying!!

116

© 2008 Precept Ministries International

LESSON TWO

1. Read Exodus 17:1-7 again to put yourself in context, then answer the following questions:

   a. Why did the people quarrel with Moses?

   b. Was it legitimate? Why or why not?

2. Moses' life offers so many lessons in leadership! Note exactly how Moses handles this situation. Record your insights below, point by point.

3. Look up the following verses to see if this was Moses' typical response to the people's grumblings over their circumstances. Note how he handles each situation.

   a. Exodus 5:15–6:9

   b. Exodus 14:10-21

c. Exodus 15:22-26

d. Exodus 16:2-9

4. Now review your observations. What did you learn from these events in Moses' life? Are there any principles, any precepts for life you can apply? Think about leadership roles you hold or might hold later. How can you follow these principles?

Who is a leader? Is the title reserved for those in official positions? If you are an older brother or sister, on a school or church council, captain of a sports team, then you are too. And one day you may be in charge of people in your workplace, church, or community. The possibilities are endless, but the responsibility is the same – to honor God in whatever position He places you.

When you look at God's response to Israel's complaints, you see His character. As the Psalmist says, "But You, O Lord, are a God merciful and gracious, slow to anger and abundant in lovingkindness and truth." (Psalm 86:15)

Do you ever grumble and complain? Are you unhappy with the way things are going in your life and blame God? Maybe you have grumbled about your parents or a teacher – those God put in charge of you. If so, then it's good for you also to know that God is slow to anger and abundant in **lovingkindness**. Take time to repent and thank Him for His patience.

© 2008 Precept Ministries International

LESSON THREE

1. Your assignment today is to look up the following scriptures, meditate on them, and write all you learn from them about the rock and the water that flowed from it and their **symbolism**.

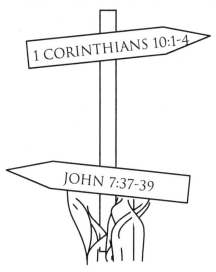

1 CORINTHIANS 10:1-4

JOHN 7:37-39

   a. What does Jesus tell the thirsty to do?

   b. What happens to the one who believes?

   c. When?

   d. When was the Spirit given? (Look at Acts 1:3-6 and 2:1-4 if you don't know.)

   e. So what had to happen to Jesus before the thirsty could drink and be satisfied with living waters? How does this relate to the rock of Exodus 17?

2. Explain in your own words what you learned about the rock.

3. Have you come to the rock? Do you believe? Do you have to thirst anymore? Think about this and write out your thoughts.

4. Finally, what can you apply to your life? Any principles to live by? Any cautions?

> God has given you a Rock from which flows living water. "He who believes in Me, as the Scripture said, 'From his innermost being will flow rivers of living water." God willl supply all of your needs according to His riches in glory through Christ Jesus our Lord. Quit complaining and drink from Christ.

  © *2008 Precept Ministries International*

LESSON FOUR

1. Finish observing Exodus 17. As you read verses 8-16, mark key words from your bookmark. Then list the main characters (including the Lord) and what you learn about them.

JEHOVAH NISSI
"THE LORD
IS OUR BANNER"

2. Look at your Observation Worksheets of chapters 4 to 17 and note every place you marked *staff*. If you gain any new insights — how it was used, who used it, when, under what circumstances, why it was used, and why — record your observations below.

3. Why did God want to blot out Amalek's memory from under heaven? Read Deuteronomy 25:17-19.

A CLOSER LOOK:

Deuteronomy records Moses' giving of the law to the generation of Israel who would enter the Promised Land. Numbers 13-14 records God's declaration that those who rebelled in the wilderness would die in the wilderness.

Genesis 36:10-12 lists Amalek as one of Esau's grandsons. So he and his descendants are relatives of the children of Israel (Jacob, Esau's brother).

THE MORE YOU KNOW...

© 2008 Precept Ministries International

LESSON FIVE

1. Read Exodus 18 carefully and mark the text. As you do, list the names of Moses' sons and why he gave them their names.

2. How did Moses influence his father-in-law Jethro?

3. How did Jethro influence Moses? Write out how Jethro advised Moses and why. Also, list each of Jethro's instructions.

4. Are there any lessons for life? Any insights on good management? God had reasons for Moses to record this for us. Can you think of any?

5. Finally, record themes for Exodus 17 and 18 on the "At A Glance" chart.

It's rich, isn't it? There is so much to be learned! Why do we entangle ourselves in worldly pursuits? Is this why the Church on the whole is more like the world than like Christ?

© *2008 Precept Ministries International*

ENRICHMENT WORDS:

Jehovah Nissi – the Lord is our banner.

Lovingkindness – God's devotion, loyalty, and covenant faithfulness.[1]

Symbolism – a picture or object that represents a fact, event, or truth.[2]

---

[1] Achtemeier, Paul J., Publishers Harper & Row, and Society of Biblical Literature. *Harper's Bible Dictionary*. 1st ed. San Francisco: Harper & Row, 1985, p. 581.
[2] Arthur, Kay. *How to Study Your Bible Precept Upon Precept*. Eugene, Oregon: Harvest House Publishers, 1995, p. 93.

© *2008 Precept Ministries International*

© *2008 Precept Ministries International*

Fear and Obey

Do you fear God? Do you honor Him? If you know Him according to His Word, then you know He is worthy of honor and reverence. So how do you reflect this in your behavior?

In this unit you'll study a nation's up-close encounter with the Living God. You'll see what standing in His presence means and what He demands of His people. And although you probably know most of the commands we'll study, you'll be challenged to think critically about their relevance today to your life, society, and nation.

Will you fear and obey the Lord?

© *2008 Precept Ministries International*

© *2008 Precept Ministries International*

LESSON ONE

1. Begin this unit by carefully reading and observing Exodus 19.

    a. Mark time references with a green clock and record the details in the margin of your Observation Worksheet. How much time has elapsed between Exodus 16:1 and 19:1?

    b. Mark references to *Mount Sinai* (also called *Horeb*) and *mountain* as you marked other geographical locations. Then ask the 5W and H questions and list what you learn about it below.

© 2008 Precept Ministries International

c. The Lord's commands to His people and their responses are very important. Mark references to the *people* in this chapter and then list your observations.

2. Finally, a question to meditate on: What did you learn about approaching God from this chapter? How can you apply these truths to your life? Write out your insights below.

Were you awed by God's power and majesty as He came down on the mountain? Does it change how you consider approaching Him in prayer and worship? He certainly isn't the "big fella upstairs" that you approach in a haphazard manner, is He? Although believers are able to enter His presence with confidence through the blood of Christ, it's still important to realize that He is God, not man. He is worthy of your respect and reverence.

© 2008 Precept Ministries International

LESSON TWO

PRECEPT
UPON
PRECEPT®

Exodus
U-7, Lesson 2, Chapter 20

1. Observe Exodus 20, marking key words including *test* and *sin*. Note how this chapter ties in with chapter 19. Also mark the key repeated phrase *the Lord your God*.

   When you finish observing this chapter, number the commandments with a pencil. Write them below to help you remember them.

2. Look up the following scriptures and note what they say about these commandments.

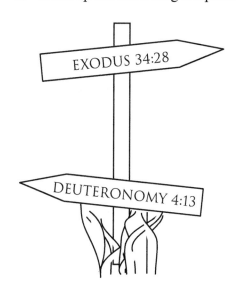

EXODUS 34:28

DEUTERONOMY 4:13

3. Now look at the commandments in Exodus 20:1-17 and see if they can be categorized or grouped according to whom and what they relate. Record your insights below.

How long has it been since you read the Ten Commandments, thought about their significance, and examined your life in light of them? Think about how you are to honor God and treat other people... how do you measure up to His standards?

© *2008 Precept Ministries International*

LESSON THREE

PRECEPT
UPON
PRECEPT.

Exodus
U-7, Lesson 3, Chapter 20

1. Are believers now licensed to break the commandments in Exodus 20? Does "under **grace**" mean you can live however you want or God changed His standard of holiness for His people? Before you go any further in this study, you need to see how the Law relates to a Christian living under grace in the New Covenant.

    Look up the following cross-references. Check the context, note who is speaking and to whom, and record what you learn about how a believer is to live, the Law, and the believer's relationship to it.

MATTHEW 5:17-20

ROMANS 8:3-4

1 JOHN 3:4-10

© 2008 Precept Ministries International

2. Considering all that you have observed, what is a Christian's relationship to the Law?

© *2008 Precept Ministries International*

LESSON FOUR

It's time to focus on the details of the Ten Commandments – your assigment for the remainder of the unit.

1. God prefaces His commandments with this statement: "I am the LORD your God, who brought you out of the land of Egypt, out of the house of slavery" (Exodus 20:2).

    a. What is the relationship between this opening statement and the first commandment (v.3)?

    b. The words "before Me" in Exodus 20:3 can be translated "besides Me." Why are there to be no other gods besides Him? Read Isaiah 42:8 and record what it says about God's glory.

2. Now look at the second commandment in Exodus 20:4-6. Can you see any connection or flow of thought from verse 2? Explain your answer.

3. What does God mean: "visiting the iniquity of the fathers on the children, on the third and the fourth generations of those who hate Me, but showing lovingkindness to thousands, to those who love Me and keep My commandments"? Deuteronomy is partially a commentary on Exodus. Here are a few verses from it that will help with this lesson.

DEUTERONOMY 24:16

   a. Scripture interprets Scripture; it never contradicts itself. What does this verse teach about the sins of fathers and sons?

© 2008 Precept Ministries International

DEUTERONOMY 6:4-12

b. Note the responsibility of the father; then think of what happens to the children when fathers fail in this responsibility. Write your insights below.

EXODUS 34:7

c. Visiting the iniquity of the fathers to the third and fourth generations is quoted in Deuteronomy 5:9 as part of the Ten Commandments and then mentioned again in the following verses. Record your insights.

NUMBERS 14:18

d. Finally, write how you would explain Exodus 20:5-6 to another person. If you don't know exactly what it *means*, can you say what it does *not mean*?

© *2008 Precept Ministries International*

e. What will you pass on to your children?

4. How can a believer be sure not to worship and serve idols?

a. Look up the following New Testament reference and record what you learn about idolatry.

COLOSSIANS 3:1-6

b. What are believers to do in this passage and why?

c. What is greed?

d. Do you have any idols in your life? If so, what should you "consider"?

© 2008 Precept Ministries International

© *2008 Precept Ministries International*

LESSON FIVE

1. How often do you hear the Lord's name used as an expletive or in profanity? What will happen to people who talk that way? Read Exodus 20:7, the third commandment, and do the following:

   a. Mark the phrase *the Lord your God*, used in conjunction with this commandment. Do you remember what you learned about the Lord in Exodus 3:13-15 and 6:2-8? Look at these passages again and think about this: if God's name encompasses what He is — His character, power, authority — what does taking His name in vain mean? (Use the definition in the pull-out box to help you answer this question.)

> A **word study** is an interpretation tool that takes you back to the original language to get the full meaning of a word. Once you discover the original meaning, you can plug it back into the text to see how it enhances your understanding. Just remember: the text always dictates the meaning of the word. Just choosing a certain definition that sounds good to you or fits a certain viewpoint is not handling God's Word accurately. Context rules!

> 7723 [*shav', shav /shawv/*]
> **Vain** (n.) – nothingness, emptiness, vanity, anything which disappoints the hope which rests upon it.[1]

   b. What do the following verses teach you about taking His name in vain?

DEUTERONOMY 28:58-59

---

[1] Spiros Zodhiates, *The Complete Word Study Old Testament* (Chattanooga, TN: AMG Publishers, 1994), H2306.

2. Read Exodus 20:8-11 again.

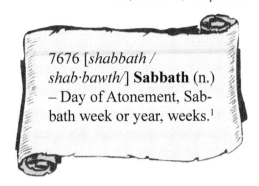

7676 [*shabbath /
shab·bawth/*] **Sabbath** (n.)
– Day of Atonement, Sab-
bath week or year, weeks.[1]

   a. If you didn't mark *sabbath*, do so now. Then read its definition.

   b. What did you learn about it from this passage? (You'll learn more when you study Exodus 31.)

   c. Keeping Exodus 20 in mind, read Deuteronomy 5:12-15. According to this passage, what's the reason for keeping the sabbath?

3. "**Honor** your father and your mother, that your days may be prolonged in the land." Interesting commandment, isn't it? It shows how much God values parents. Can you imagine the change in society if this commandment were kept?

   a. Look up the following passages and note what you learn about parents and God's blessing.

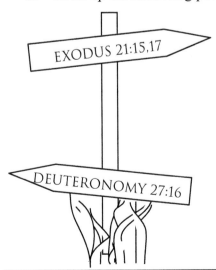

EXODUS 21:15,17

DEUTERONOMY 27:16

---

[1] Strong, James. *The Exhaustive Concordance of the Bible : Showing Every Word of the Text of the Common English Version of the Canonical Books, and Every Occurrence of Each Word in Regular Order.* electronic ed. Ontario: Woodside Bible Fellowship., 1996, H7676.

© *2008 Precept Ministries International*

Notice how Exodus 20 is restated to those living under the New Covenant.

b. There are more Scriptures on this subject, but this is adequate for our study. Now hold up the mirror of the Word and take a good, honest look at yourself and how you have treated your parents. Do you measure up to God's standard or have you adopted the world's traditions? Write our your answer so you can see it.

© 2008 Precept Ministries International

© *2008 Precept Ministries International*

LESSON SIX

1. "You shall not murder" (Exodus 20:13). Read the Hebrew word for "murder" (kill, KJV). Then read the following cross-references and record what you learn about it.

7523 [*ratsach /raw·tsakh/*] **Murder** (v.) – To kill a human being, murder, slay, commit manslaughter, to destroy, crush.[1]

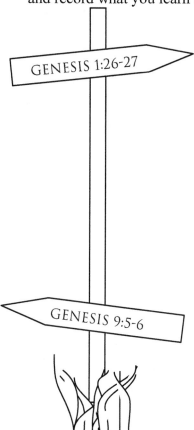

GENESIS 1:26-27

GENESIS 9:5-6

2. "You shall not commit adultery." How pertinent is this command for our times? Read the Hebrew word for adultery, then the following verses and see what you learn from them.

5003 [*na'aph /naw·af/*] **Adultery** (v.) – sexual intercourse with the wife or betrothed of another man.[2]

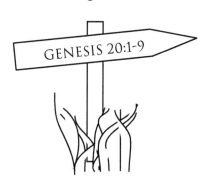

GENESIS 20:1-9

---

[1] Spiros Zodhiates, *The Complete Word Study Old Testament* (Chattanooga, TN: AMG Publishers, 1994), H7523.
[2] R. Laird Harris, Robert Laird Harris, Gleason Leonard Archer and Bruce K. Waltke, *Theological Wordbook of the Old Testament*, electronic ed. (Chicago: Moody Press, 1999, c1980). 542.

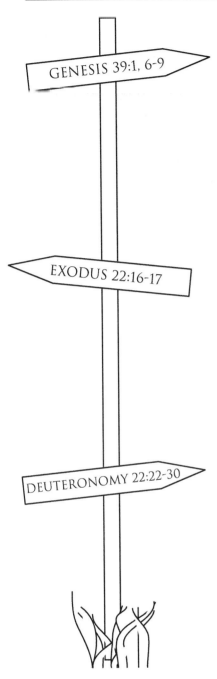

3. How serious is God about adultery? Is adultery viewed the same way today?

© 2008 Precept Ministries International

4. Now, look at the definition for covet, and then the cross-references below. Record what you learn.

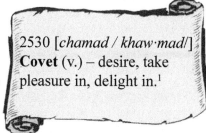

2530 [*chamad / khaw·mad/*]
Covet (v.) – desire, take pleasure in, delight in.[1]

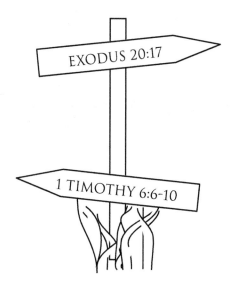

EXODUS 20:17

a. What are you not to covet? List the items.

1 TIMOTHY 6:6-10

b. What can you learn from these verses to keep you from coveting?

5. Finally, what do you learn about believers from this passage? In light of these verses and other cross-references in this lesson, what changes do you need to ask God to make in your thinking and behavior?

EPHESIANS 4:17-32

> So where do you stand in regard to these commands – with God or the world? You can't honor God and agree with what the world says about lying, murder, adultery and coveting. Who will you choose to follow?

[1] Robert L. Thomas, *New American Standard Hebrew-Aramaic and Greek Dictionaries: Updated Edition* (Anaheim: Foundation Publications, Inc., 1998, 1981). H2530.

© 2008 Precept Ministries International

© *2008 Precept Ministries International*

LESSON SEVEN

PRECEPT
UPON
PRECEPT®

Exodus
U-7, Lesson 7, Chapter 20

1. It must have been an awesome experience to stand at the foot of Sinai as God gave the Law.

    a. Read Exodus 20:18-21. Record what you learn about the people's response.

    b. Why did God appear to the people as He did?

    c. Based on what you saw in these verses, why do people disobey God's commands today?

2. Finish this unit by reading the scriptures in the sign post. Note that "the words" in Deuteronomy 5:22 refer to the Ten Commandments reiterated in verses 1-21.

DEUTERONOMY 5:1–6:25

Read these passages thoughtfully. Meditate on them. Let the truths seep deep into your heart, then ask God to seal them there. Grace does not make us lawless; rather it enables us to keep the Law. When you finish, write out what you learned that you can apply to your life. What warning is God giving you in these verses?

3.   Record themes for Exodus 19 and 20 on the "At A Glance" chart.

© *2008 Precept Ministries International*

ENRICHMENT WORDS:

Adultery – physical or mental sex with anyone other than your spouse.

Covet – desire, take pleasure in, delight in.[1]

Grace – unmerited favor.

Honor – give weight; esteem.[2]

Murder – the crime of unlawfully killing a person especially with malice.

Vain – nothingness, emptiness, vanity, anything which disappoints the hope which rests upon it.[3]

---

[1] c.f. p. 145
[2] Spiros Zodhiates, *The Complete Word Study Old Testament* (Chattanooga, TN: AMG Publishers, 1994), H3513.
[3] c.f. p.139

© *2008 Precept Ministries International*

© *2008 Precept Ministries International*

When God Sets the Standard

Have you ever wondered what it would be like if God governed our nation... if we lived under a theocratic form of government rather than a democratic one? What would the laws of the land be like?

In Exodus 20, God lays out His Ten Commandments succinctly, telling His people what they are and are not to do. Now in Exodus 21-23, God explains how they are to practically apply these laws to their lives.

Did you know He is so interested in men's daily affairs that He laid out ordinances to govern every area of their lives? What you'll discover in Exodus is just the beginning; Leviticus goes into more detail. God wants His people to live "set apart," to be holy. You'll get a glimpse of what holy living is – God's standard for righteousness and justice.

© 2008 Precept Ministries International

LESSON ONE

The first three lessons of this unit will focus on observing Exodus 21-23.

1. Begin by observing Exodus 21.

    a. Mark words from your bookmark and include the the following:

        1)   **ordinance** with stone tablets like this ⌒

        2)   *redeemed* with a green **$**

        3)   *death* with a tombstone like this ⌂

    b. Note paragraph divisions that deal with particular laws in the margin of your Observation Worksheet, for example: servitude, homicide, bodily injury, property damage, etc.

    c. List the action to be taken in each situation in the margin of your Observation Worksheet.

        2. Record a theme for chapter 21 on the "At A Glance" chart.

3. Which of the Ten Commandments are explained in detail in this chapter?

4. Think about what you have learned in your study on Exodus.

    a. Were the sons of Israel familiar with slavery? How?

    b. How are these ordinances different from what they experienced?

    c. Why does God tell a people familiar with slavery how to treat slaves?

© 2008 Precept Ministries International

d. Is there anything you can apply to your life from your observations on God? What thinking have you learned from the world that you need to "transform"?

> "And do not be conformed to this world, but be transformed by the renewing of your mind, so that you may prove what the will of God is, that which is good and acceptable and perfect."
> - Romans 12:2

GOD'S LAW VERSUS MAN'S

For this project you need:

Magazines   Newspapers   Internet

Find a current event that details one of the crimes listed in Exodus 21. Summarize the article and how it relates to the crime listed in Exodus. If a verdict has been determined, explain whether it fits with God's judgment. If a verdict has not been decided, explain what God's judgment is based on Exodus 21. If the article doesn't give enough information, explain what evidence is needed to determine God's judgment.

© 2008 Precept Ministries International

LESSON TWO

1. Observe Exodus 22.

    a. Mark words from your bookmark and include **restitution** and its synonym *payment*.

  b. Note paragraph divisions that deal with particular laws in the margin of your Observation Worksheet.

    c. List the action to be taken in each situation in the margin of your Observation Worksheet.

    2. Record a theme for chapter 22 on the "At A Glance" chart.

3. Which of the Ten Commandments are explained in detail?

4. What did you learn about God in this chapter? Are you living according to His standards? How have the ordinances in this chapter transformed your thinking?

Do you understand your relationship to the Law? Do you evaluate your behavior according to God's Word? This is the only way to know if you are pleasing God in all you do. Study diligently to know the full counsel of God's Word so you can honor Him.

© 2008 Precept Ministries International

© 2008 Precept Ministries International

LESSON THREE

1. Observe Exodus 23.

    a. Mark words from your bookmark.

    b. Note paragraph divisions that deal with particular laws in the margin of your Observation Worksheet.

    c. List the action to be taken in each situation in the margin of your Observation Worksheet.

    2. Record a theme for chapter 23 on the "At A Glance" chart.

3. Which of the Ten Commandments are explained in detail in this chapter?

4. God lists several things in verses 1-9 that should not influence a person's behavior or decisions. List them below. Then think about what influences your behavior and decisions – is there anything your need to change?

5. What are the people *not* to do according to 23:13? What are they to do according to 23:14?

    a. How do these verses connect? How would the instruction in verse 14 help them keep the command in verse 13?

© 2008 Precept Ministries International

b. How can you apply this same principle to your life?

6. Look at Exodus 23:20-33.

   a. What are God's instructions to the people?

   b. What will God do if the children of Israel obey these commands?

7. Although believers are not given exactly the same instructions or promises, what do you learn about obedience from these verses?

© *2008 Precept Ministries International*

8. Now reflect on what your nation would be like if it were a theocracy. Would the individual have greater protection? Would your society fair better or worse? Why? Would the judicial system function differently? How?

© *2008 Precept Ministries International*

1. Exodus 24 is an extremely important chapter so observe it very carefully.

    a.   Mark the words from your key word bookmark. Add *blood* as a key word and mark it with three red dots. Also, don't forget to mark references to time.

    b. Look at what the chapter is about and summarize it in one sentence.

    c. List the main characters and what the text tells you about them.

2. In the margin of your Observation Worksheet, record the names of individuals in this chapter who are not main characters. As you read through the **Torah** (the first five books of the Bible) these names will appear again and you want to know who they are. For example, Joshua has an entire book named after him.

3. Illustrate the progression of events in this chapter in the boxes on the following page; it will help you remember them. Be creative!

© *2008 Precept Ministries International*

EXODUS 24:1-2

EXODUS 24:3

EXODUS 24:4-5

EXODUS 24:6-8

EXODUS 24:9-11

EXODUS 24:12

© 2008 Precept Ministries International

EXODUS 24:13-14

EXODUS 24:15-16

EXODUS 24:17-18

© 2008 Precept Ministries International

© *2008 Precept Ministries International*

LESSON FIVE

Today you'll look at cross-references that will help you interpret Exodus 24. First, you'll look at Moses' role in the covenant cut in Exodus 24, then what the New Testament tells you about it. However, you won't study this topic exhaustively because Exodus is long and there is a lot to cover in the remaining three units.

1285 [*bâriyth /ber·eeth/*]
Covenant (n.) – a compact (...made by passing between pieces of flesh): confederacy, covenant, league.[1]

1. Look up the following verses and record what you learn about Moses and his relationship to the covenant that was cut in Exodus 24:

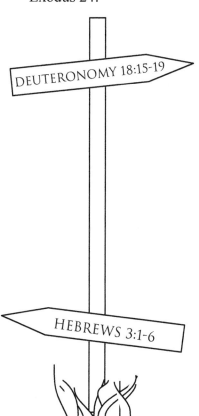

DEUTERONOMY 18:15-19

HEBREWS 3:1-6

a.   Moses is telling the people what God told him. List what God says He will do.

b.   Record what you learn about Moses. Also, don't miss the contrast between Moses and Jesus Christ. Think about how this parallels with what you observed in Deuteronomy 18.

---

[1] Spiros Zodhiates, *The Complete Word Study Old Testament* (Chattanooga, TN: AMG Publishers, 1994), H7523.

© 2008 Precept Ministries International

2. Now read Hebrews 9:18-20, printed out below. Mark references to *blood* as you did previously and *covenant* with a yellow box shaded red.

HEBREWS 9:18-20

18 Therefore even the first *covenant* was not inaugurated without blood.

19 For when every commandment had been spoken by Moses to all the people according to the Law, he took the blood of the calves and the goats, with water and scarlet wool and hyssop, and sprinkled both the book itself and all the people, saying, "THIS IS THE BLOOD OF THE COVENANT WHICH GOD COMMANDED YOU."

3. Now, what covenant does this passage in Hebrews refer to? And where can you read about it – what book and chapter?

> There's more to see in Hebrews about the covenant, but you'll look at it in the next unit when you study the tabernacle's construction and its furnishings. The imagery is awesome!
>
> You are done for today, but there is more to learn from Exodus 24 in the next lesson.

© 2008 Precept Ministries International

LESSON SIX

PRECEPT
UPON
PRECEPT®

Exodus
U-8, Lesson 6, Chapter 24

1. Take a moment to look at the meal eaten in Exodus 24:11. It was common practice to share a meal when a covenant was made. Compare the following references and note your observations. Mark references to *covenant* since everything God does is based on covenant.

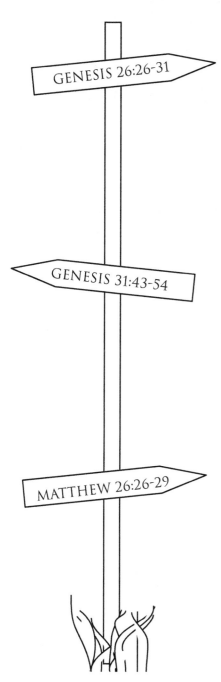

GENESIS 26:26-31

GENESIS 31:43-54

MATTHEW 26:26-29

2. How solemn was the covenant cut that day when the children of Israel vowed to keep God's words, God's commandments? Hebrews 2:1-3 tells you. In pointing out the gravity of holding on to their faith in Christ and the covenant inaugurated in His blood, God reminds His readers of the Old Covenant, the Law, inaugurated in Exodus 24.

   Read Hebrews 2:1-3 and see how it relates in gravity to what you have just studied in Exodus 21–24. Write your comments below.

3. What did you learn about the covenant made in Exodus 24 and the New Covenant made through Jesus Christ from the cross-references in the last two lessons? How serious is the decision to enter into the New Covenant? Is it something to take lightly, something more than a one-time prayer? Record your thoughts.

 1. Record a theme for chapter 24 on the "At A Glance" chart.

© *2008 Precept Ministries International*

Hebrews 12:18-25 says:

"For you have not come to a mountain that may be touched and to a blazing fire, and to darkness and gloom and whirlwind, and to the blast of a trumpet and the sound of words which sound was such that those who heard begged that no further word should be spoken to them.

For they could not bear the command, 'If even a beast touches the mountain, it will be stoned.'

And so terrible was the sight, that Moses said, 'I am full of fear and trembling.'

But you have come to Mount Zion and to the city of the living God, the heavenly Jerusalem, and to myriads of angels, to the general assembly and church of the first-born who are enrolled in heaven, and to God, the Judge of all, and to the spirits of righteous men made perfect, and to Jesus, the mediator of a new covenant, and to the sprinkled blood, which speaks better than the blood of Abel.

See to it that you do not refuse Him who is speaking. For if those did not escape when they refused him who warned them on earth, much less shall we escape who turn away from Him who warns from heaven."

Meditate on this poignant passage. How well it depicts the events in Exodus and the seriousness of entering into a covenant with the Living God. Now what does God require of you?

He has told you, O man, what is good;
And what does the Lord require of you
But to do justice, to love kindness,
And to walk humbly with your God? (Micah 6:8)

© *2008 Precept Ministries International*

ENRICHMENT WORDS:

Covenant – a contract, legal pledges between two parties with consequences related to compliances and non compliances.

Ordinance – law, rule, custom, manner.[1]

Restitution – repayment over and above the actual loss; punitive damages.[2]

Torah – the five books of Moses; the Pentateuch.

---

[1] Spiros Zodhiates, *The Complete Word Study Old Testament* (Chattanooga, TN: AMG Publishers, 1994), H4941.
[2] Achtemeier, Paul J., Publishers Harper & Row and Society of Biblical Literature. *Harper's Bible Dictionary*. 1st ed. San Francisco: Harper & Row, 1985, p. 863.

© 2008 Precept Ministries International

Exodus
U-8, Chapters 21-24

© *2008 Precept Ministries International*

Worshipping a Holy God

How do you worship a holy God?

Is it up to you? Can people worship God any way they want? Is that really worship?

Many people try to worship God on their terms, in ways that satisfy their needs and desires. It's important that you to look at God's Word for yourself to understand what He demands of His followers – true worship.

© 2008 Precept Ministries International

© *2008 Precept Ministries International*

LESSON ONE

Exodus 25:1-9 introduces what follows to the end of Exodus.

1. Read this passage and mark words from your key word bookmark and include:

    a.   ***contribution***

    b.   ***tabernacle***, *sanctuary* or *tent of meeting*

2. Now list on the following chart what you learned about the *contribution* and the *tabernacle*. Don't forget to ask the 5W and H questions!

> This is the first of 139 uses of the word "tabernacle" — "mishkan" in Hebrew. "Mishkan" means "a dwelling place." The tabernacle is the place where God dwells.
>
> Sanctuary translates the Hebrew "miqdash," meaning "a place set apart, holy."

THE CONTRIBUTION	THE TABERNACLE

© 2008 Precept Ministries International

3. To fully appreciate what you are about to see, read Hebrews 7:22–8:5. The main point is in Hebrews 8:5; but when you read from Hebrews 7:22, you get a glimpse of the substance of the shadow — Jesus Christ and the things in the heavens. As you read, mark references to *covenant* as you did previously.

HEBREWS 7:22-8:5

22   so much the more also Jesus has become the guarantee of a better covenant.

23   The former priests, on the one hand, existed in greater numbers because they were prevented by death from continuing,

24   but Jesus, on the other hand, because He continues forever, holds His priesthood permanently.

25   Therefore He is able also to save forever those who draw near to God through Him, since He always lives to make intercession for them.

26   For it was fitting for us to have such a high priest, holy, innocent, undefiled, separated from sinners and exalted above the heavens;

27   who does not need daily, like those high priests, to offer up sacrifices, first for His own sins and then for the sins of the people, because this He did once for all when He offered up Himself.

28   For the Law appoints men as high priests who are weak, but the word of the oath, which came after the Law, appoints a Son, made perfect forever.

8:1   Now the main point in what has been said is this: we have such a high priest, who has taken His seat at the right hand of the throne of the Majesty in the heavens,

2   a minister in the sanctuary and in the true tabernacle, which the Lord pitched, not man.

3   For every high priest is appointed to offer both gifts and sacrifices; so it is necessary that this high priest also have something to offer.

4   Now if He were on earth, He would not be a priest at all, since there are those who offer the gifts according to the Law;

5   who serve a copy and shadow of the heavenly things, just as Moses was warned by God when he was about to erect the tabernacle; for, "SEE," He says, "THAT YOU MAKE all things ACCORDING TO THE PATTERN WHICH WAS SHOWN YOU ON THE MOUNTAIN."

   © *2008 Precept Ministries International*

a.   What role does Jesus hold, according to 8:1?

b.   Where does He minister? How was this place made?

c.   What do you learn about the tabernacle Moses built according to verse 5? What was it patterned after?

> Do you understand that your careful study of the tabernacle and priesthood will not only give you a picture of Christ but also what the heavenly throne room looks like? That's pretty amazing isn't it?

© 2008 Precept Ministries International

LESSON TWO

Today you will finish observing Exodus 25, then observe chapters 26 and 27.

1. Read Exodus 25-27.

    a. Mark words from your key word bookmark.

    b. As each piece of furniture or part of the tabernacle is introduced, write it in the margin of your Observation Worksheet next to the verses that detail its construction. This will help you remember what the text says and prepare you for a later assignment.

© *2008 Precept Ministries International*

LESSONS THREE & FOUR

This lesson will take two days to complete so do as much as you can the first day and finish the next.

1. You will find drawings of each piece of furniture below, based on the illustrations in the *Inductive Study Bible*.

   a. Next to each piece, list where it's placed in the tabernacle, what it's made of, and what its purpose is (if given).

   b. Under each piece, you will find one or more scriptures to look up. Some will give further details about the purpose of each piece, others help you see what the earthly shadow represents in heaven. After you look up the cross-references, write down additional insights they give and answer the question:"What was the _____ a shadow of?"

ARK AND MERCY SEAT

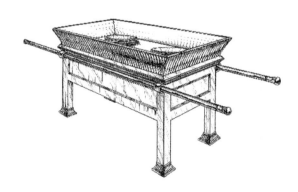

PLACEMENT:

MATERIALS:

PURPOSE:

HEBREWS 9:3-9

TABLE OF SHOWBREAD

PLACEMENT:

MATERIALS:

PURPOSE:

JOHN 6:51

© 2008 Precept Ministries International

LAMPSTAND

PLACEMENT:

MATERIALS:

PURPOSE:

REVELATION 4:5

JOHN 1:9; 8:12

REVELATION 21:22-23

THE CURTAINS

PLACEMENT:

MATERIALS:

PURPOSE:

This view shows each layer of coverings drawn back to reveal the layer beneath.

© 2008 Precept Ministries International

THE VEIL

PLACEMENT:

MATERIALS:

PURPOSE:

JOHN 14:6:

MATTHEW 27:51:

HEBREWS 10:19-20

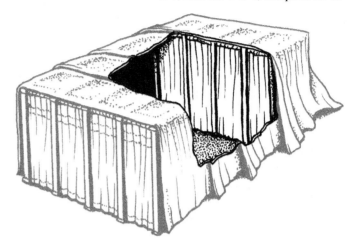

This cutaway view shows the veil inside the tabernacle.

BRONZE ALTAR

PLACEMENT:

MATERIALS:

PURPOSE:

HEBREWS 10:10-12 (1-12)

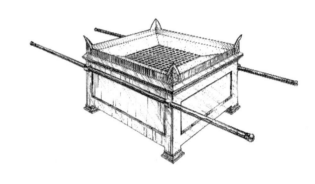

2. Record themes for chapters 25-27 on the "At A Glance" chart.

> Did you realize how significant the tabernacle is to you, a believer under the New Covenant of Grace? When you understand the tabernacle and the purposes for its parts, you understand more about Jesus and what He has done on your behalf! You also get an amazing glimpse of what is in heaven! These chapters may seem monotonous at first, but hopefully you have now seen how important they are for you to understand typology in the Old Covenant.

© *2008 Precept Ministries International*

1. Today you will look at Exodus 28. Begin with the first five introductory verses.

   a. List the people mentioned in the first five verses and note who they are.

   b. What is to be done? For whom?

   c. List the garments to be made.

   d. What will the garments be made from and where will the material come from? (Compare Exodus 28 with Exodus 25:1-9.)

© 2008 Precept Ministries International

2. The sons of Israel were enslaved 400 years. Where did they get the resources for the contribution for the tabernacle and the garments? Read Exodus 3:21-22 and 12:35-36.

3. Now read Exodus 28 and mark key words.

    a. Add *die* to your key word list. Mark it with a black tombstone like this: ▐.

    b. Each time a description of a garment is given, write the name of the garment in the margin so you can divide the chapter according to the garments.

4. Look at the pictures of the high priest and his garments to get a visual picture of the description given in this chapter.

THE EPHOD   THE BREASTPIECE

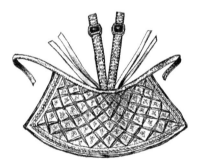   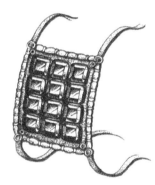

THE TURBAN

          © *2008 Precept Ministries International*

THE ROBE OF THE EPHOD

You should have good visual pictures of the garments by the time you finish this lesson. If you can't appreciate this now, you will later when you come across passages like Judges 18 where the Danites steal an ephod! You will know what an ephod is! The Holy Spirit will bring it back to mind because you were faithful.

© 2008 Precept Ministries International

LESSON SIX

1. Exodus 29 begins with: "Now this is what you shall do to them to consecrate them to minister as priests to Me." By way of introduction, look up the following verses and record what you learn. They will make this chapter more interesting and applicable. Note by each reference who is being described and how.

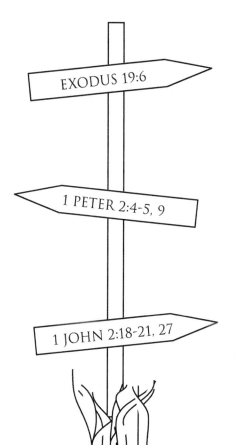

EXODUS 19:6

1 PETER 2:4-5, 9

1 JOHN 2:18-21, 27

Mark *anointing* and record what you learn about the children of God. (Look at John 14:26 to see who this anointing is.)

2. Now in light of these cross-references, carefully read the instructions for the priests and remember that believers fulfill this role under the New Covenant. Believers are set apart for service as they were. Although you won't be sacrificing animals or burning incense, you will be serving the Lord and ministering to others. How does this change your thinking and affect your behavior?

3. Now read Exodus 29 and, in addition to the words on your list, mark the following key words including synonyms and pronouns:

   a. ***anoint***

   b. ***ordain*** (*ordination*)

c. *offerings* (e.g. sin offering, burnt offering, etc.)

4. Your final assignment today is to observe Exodus 30 and mark key words. In the margin of your worksheet, note what each paragraph covers. Then list next to each drawing of the furniture below where it was to be placed in the tabernacle, what it's made of, and what its purpose is (if its given).

ALTAR OF INCENSE

PLACEMENT:

MATERIALS:

PURPOSE:

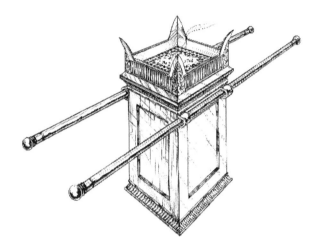

BRONZE LAVER

PLACEMENT:

MATERIALS:

PURPOSE:

© *2008 Precept Ministries International*

LESSON SEVEN

1. Read Exodus 31:1-11.

   a. Mark words from your key word bookmark.

   b. List below what this passage teaches you about the following:

BEZALEL	OHOLIAB	THE LORD

All the items the children of Israel possessed came from the Lord and were used in His service! Beyond material possessions, the Lord gave Bezalel and Oholiab talents too. All gifts are from the Lord to be used to glorify Him.

2. Now look up the following verses that describe believers. See how they compare with what you have learned about the Lord.

JOHN 15:16

© 2008 Precept Ministries International

a. God gives every believer gifts and abilities to serve Him and the body of Christ. Are you serving? If not, why not? Think about this in light of what you learned in this lesson and record your thoughts.

b. What materials and talents has the Lord given you to serve others for His glory?

© *2008 Precept Ministries International*

LESSON EIGHT

1. Read Exodus 31:12-18.

    a. Mark references to the *sabbath* including pronouns.

    b. Mark other words including *sign* from your key word bookmark.

    c. List everything you learned about the sabbath.

2. Let's take a quick look at some New Testament references to the sabbath. Record your insights next to each verse.

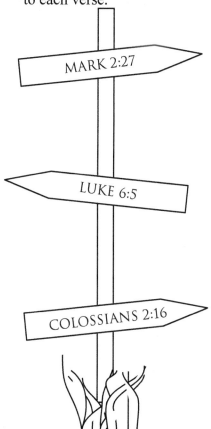

© 2008 Precept Ministries International

ROMANS 14:4-12

3. Exodus 31 says the sabbath was a sign.

   a. A sign to whom?

   b. A sign of what?

Some believe the sabbath is a sign of the coming millennial rest to be enjoyed by those who believe Jesus is the Messiah. It is a complicated study that presumes you are aware of the millennium, which is prophesied in multiple places. In Revelation 20:1-7, it's referred to six times.

4. Finally, what do you believe about keeping the sabbath?

   a. Why?

   b. How should you treat those who disagree with you? Why?

5. It's interesting to note that after God gives His commands about the sabbath, He is finished speaking. Read Exodus 31:18 again and record what God gives Moses.

6. Record themes for chapters 28-31 on the "At A Glance" chart.

© 2008 Precept Ministries International

ENRICHMENT WORDS:

Anoint – cover a body or object with oil or ointment to signify divine sanctification and approval or consecrate someone or something for a holy purpose.[1]

Contribution – payment imposed by military, civil, or ecclesiastical authorities usually for a special or extraordinary purpose.

Ordain – receive authority from God to perform special religious duties.[2]

Tabernacle – literally "to dwell;" the portable sanctuary the Israelites carried in the wilderness.[3]

---

[1] Achtemeier, Paul J., Publishers Harper & Row and Society of Biblical Literature. *Harper's Bible Dictionary*. 1st ed. San Francisco: Harper & Row, 1985, p.32.

[2] Ibid., p.733.

[3] Ibid., p.734.

© 2008 Precept Ministries International

© *2008 Precept Ministries International*

UNIT TEN

Culture's Impact

Syncretism. You may not know what it is, but you've probably experienced it. Syncretism is an attempt to reconcile opposite tenets, doctrines, and practices.

Many people, even those who call themselves Christians, support a blend of ideals, beliefs, and practices. Sadly, an even larger majority practice syncretism and don't even realize it. They don't know God's Word and don't realize they're distorting true worship with worldly and pagan practices.

In this unit you'll see how the children of Israel mixed Egyptian pagan practices with their worship. As you study this part of Exodus look at the consequences of their behavior. Then think about this question: is Christianity today impacting culture or is culture impacting Christianity?

© 2008 Precept Ministries International

© *2008 Precept Ministries International*

LESSON ONE

In the midst of this final segment on worship is a startling account of people who weeks earlier covenanted with God. They understood the covenant, the ordinances set before them were clearly recounted, and they unanimously agreed to obey.

Your assignment for today is a simple one. Read Exodus 32. Don't stop to mark the text. Read it as an eyewitness account of a historical event. Picture it in your mind. Feel the heat of God's anger. When you finish, sit for a while and contemplate what you have read.

1. Read Exodus 24:18.

   a. How long is Moses on Mount Sinai?

   b. How do the people's respond to this in Exodus 32?

> Think about what the people did — their impatience with God; the fickleness of their affections; the insanity of their request. Think about Aaron's response – his self-justification. Imagine the dismay of Moses. Watch how he handles himself, what is uppermost in his mind, and how he intercedes for the people with God. These are real people, like us, in a most alarming situation.
>
> Then ask yourself if you see any parallels between these people who were to be a holy nation and a kingdom of priests, and the church of Jesus Christ, which is designated "a kingdom, priests to His God and Father" (Revelation 1:6).

© 2008 Precept Ministries International

© *2008 Precept Ministries International*

LESSON TWO

1. Complete your observations of Exodus 32.

   a.   Mark key words from your bookmark and look for new repeated words. For example, it's important to mark the *golden calf* and its synonyms and pronouns.

   b.   Mark geographical locations and references to time.

   c.   Mark references to the people.

2.   When you finish, list everything you learn about the people and the golden calf in the chart on the following page. Star actions that violated commands God gave them 40 days earlier. Then write the commandments they broke.

3. Note the progression of events and record them in the margin of the text. When you finish, list below the main things that occurred in the order they happened.

4. Do you remember where the sons of Israel got the gold to make the calf? If not, look back at Exodus 12:35-36 and record what you learn.

© *2008 Precept Ministries International*

THE PEOPLE	THE GOLDEN CALF

© 2008 Precept Ministries International

Have you seen people grow tried of waiting on God to act? When what they wanted didn't happen when they thought it should, they took matters into their own hands? They acted rashly — maybe even contrary to what they professed to believe, contrary to the precepts of God? Where did it lead them? Maybe you've even done that yourself.

The results can be grave... and hard to live with. But as you saw when God laid down His ordinances, there are consequences.

Think about it; learn from it. This is application.

© *2008 Precept Ministries International*

LESSON THREE

1. Read the verses in the signpost – it's a good way to review what you studied yesterday.

   a. Now compare these verses and what happened in Exodus 32 with the following verses from Romans. Record your insights.

   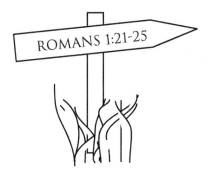

   b. What did you learn about Moses from the psalm?

2. Moses' examples show us a lot about leadership. Read Exodus 32 again and list what you learn from observing Moses in this situation. Make sure you note how he approaches God. How does he appeal to God to change His mind about harming the people?

3. Write down what you learned about Aaron's leadership. Compare his actions with Moses'.

A CLOSER LOOK AT LEVI:

The Levites' choice to stand with the Lord is the basis of their esteemed state throughout Israel's history. In Moses' blessings on the tribes in Deuteronomy 33:8-11, the Levites are praised for their zeal for the Lord in the golden calf incident. They considered God's glory before other relationships. And though Aaron and his sons are charged to minister as priests to the Lord in Exodus, the whole tribe is later set apart for God's service in Leviticus and Numbers.

THE MORE YOU KNOW...

   © *2008 Precept Ministries International*

LESSON FOUR

1. Read Exodus 32:25-35 again. What do you think about what happens? What do you think about God? What does it teach you about Him?

2. What does this entire chapter teach you about God? Record your insights from Exodus 32 in your "Journal on God."

3. Now in case you missed it, what do you see about sin in this passage? Can Moses cover the people's sins? Would blotting Moses out of God's book cover their sin?

4. What book is Moses talking about? Look at the following cross-references on various recordings. Write your insights next to each reference.

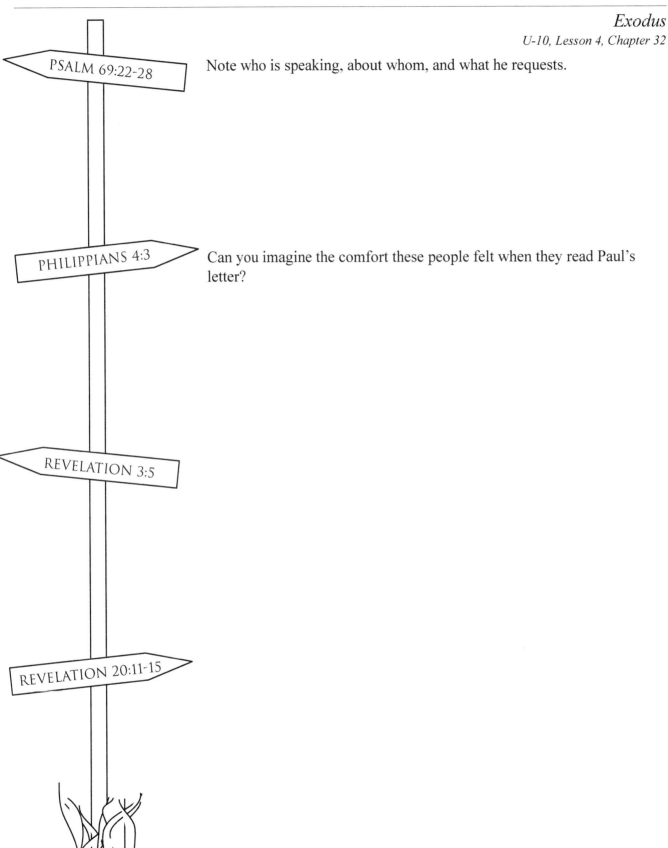

PSALM 69:22-28

Note who is speaking, about whom, and what he requests.

PHILIPPIANS 4:3

Can you imagine the comfort these people felt when they read Paul's letter?

REVELATION 3:5

REVELATION 20:11-15

© 2008 Precept Ministries International

5. From what you learned in Exodus 32 and the cross-references, what does Moses ask God to do to his name?

   a. What does this tell you about Moses as a leader?

   b. How does God respond to Moses?

   c. Can you know if your name is written in this book?

   d. What will happen to those whose names are not written in this book?

> Well, what about you? Is your name in the book? If so, take time to thank God. If you're unsure, take time to consider if you want your name in the book. Don't hesitate to find a parent or teacher and talk to them about how you can be sure your name is in the book of life.

© 2008 Precept Ministries International

© 2008 Precept Ministries International

LESSON FIVE

1. Exodus 33 is an awesome chapter. Read it carefully; don't hurry. Mark key words including the phrase *My glory* or *Thy glory*.

2. Did you notice the interlude between verses 6 and 12? What insight do these verses give you on Moses? Write below what you learn about his leadership.

3. What does Moses want from God? How does he attain it? Record your answers below.

WHAT MOSES WANTS FROM GOD	THE BASIS OF HIS REQUEST

4. Why do you think Moses found favor in God's sight? What can you learn from his relationship with God and how can you apply it to your life?

© 2008 Precept Ministries International

5. Record anything new that you learned about the Lord from this chapter in your "Journal on God."

6. Record themes for Exodus 32 and 33 on your "At A Glance" chart.

7. If you were sharing truths from this chapter with someone else, what kind of practical application would you suggest for their lives? What questions would you ask them, what points should they consider? Write them below.

8. Finally, consider what you wrote above. Do you need to apply these same things to your life? Do it; you will have a greater sense of God's presence – His "well-done." Obedience out of love and respect for God brings sweet confidence to our lives.

© *2008 Precept Ministries International*

ENRICHMENT WORDS:

Atone – to cover, purge, make reconciliation for sin.[1]

Syncretism – the combination of different forms of belief or practice.

---

[1] Strong, James: *The Exhaustive Concordance of the Bible: Showing Every Word of the Text of the Common English Version of the Canonical Books, and Every Occurrence of Each Word in Regular Order*. electronic ed. Ontario : Woodside Bible Fellowship., 1996, S. H3722

© 2008 Precept Ministries International

Exodus
U-10, Chapters 32-33

A Heart For God

Well done! You've come to the last unit in your study on Exodus – its final chapters about a nation set apart by the one true God. And what will you walk away with? What truths have you learned that are transforming the way you think and live? How will your relationship with God change now that you understand more about His ways and character?

And what about His friend Moses... from his encounter at the burning bush to his standing in the midst of God's glory. What insight on faith, dependence on God, and leadership can you practically apply to your life?

As you conclude your study, watch for the phrase, "He did just as the Lord had commanded..." You will see the blessings of obedience, the magnificent grace of God, and His glorious presence with His people. These final chapters will bring closure to the turbulent events in the last unit and lead you, perhaps, to see God's grace in your life in a deeper way.

ONE ON ONE:

Ask God to make you sensitive to truth. Tell Him you want to know Him through His Word and you want Him to strengthen you to give the remaining portion of Exodus your full attention. Pray that He will so capture your heart that it will be said of you, like Moses, that you did as the Lord commanded.

© 2008 Precept Ministries International

1. You will spend two days studying Exodus 34 because it's such an important chapter. You will notice that God repeats many things He has already said. So don't miss these important points He reemphasizes!

       a.   Observe and mark the text.

       b.   *Covenant* and *feasts* are mentioned again. Mark both as you did previously

       c. Watch for Moses' location and don't forget to mark *mountain* and the *cloud*.

2. Read Exodus 34:1-8 again. List the Lord's commands to Moses and his response.

3. What do you learn about the Lord from Exodus 34:1-7? Review what you learned about God's name and note how it's used here.

4. Think about when this event occurs, what events it follows. Why does God give these instructions to Moses again? What does this tell you about God? Record your insights below.

© 2008 Precept Ministries International

Have you ever sinned and regretted it because it grieved God and hurt your testimony? Does it weigh on you? Does it torment you?

The children of Israel made and worshipped an idol while Moses was on the mountain receiving God's commands. And yet, what does God saw in Exodus 34? He tells them He is compassionate and gracious, slow to anger, and abounding in lovingkindness and truth. He also tells them He forgives iniquity, transgression and sin. Maybe you need to be reminded of this too.

Embrace God's character. He doesn't want His children to live in defeat and despair. Believe in Him.

© 2008 Precept Ministries International

LESSON TWO

1. Look at how many times *covenant* is mentioned in Exodus 34. List below everything you learned from marking it.

2. Why does God mention *covenant* again? What does Moses ask God to do?

3. When you wrote what you learned about covenant, did you list why God commanded the sons of Israel not to covenant with the inhabitants of the land? List God's reasons below.

Did you mark "land" as you did before? Remember, God promised this land to Abraham, Isaac, and Jacob as an everlasting possession.

Exodus
U-11, Lesson 2, Chapter 34

4. List what you learned from marking *feasts*. Examine each reference by asking the 5W and H questions to get the *who*, *what*, *when*, *where*, *why*, and *how* of the feasts.

FEAST: _____

DETAILS:

FEAST: _____

DETAILS:

© 2008 Precept Ministries International

5. Look up the feasts mentioned in Exodus 34 on "The Feasts of Israel" chart at the end of this unit. Note the months they're celebrated and the times the people are to go to the feasts. Be sure to note the prophetic nature of these feasts – God gives us a picture of His workings with the children of Israel.

JEALOUS GOD

For this project you will need:
Bible

In Exodus 34:14, God's name is "Jealous." Look at the definition for this Hebrew word below, then read the following passages. Record what you learn from its usage and context.

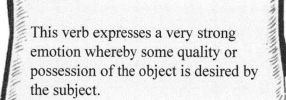

Jealous [*qana'* /ka·**na**/] – to be zealous.[1]

This verb expresses a very strong emotion whereby some quality or possession of the object is desired by the subject.

- Exodus 20:5
- Numbers 25:11
- Deuteronomy 4:24; 5:9; 6:15; 32:16, 21
- Joshua 24:19
- Ezekiel 39:25
- Nahum 1:2

Now summarize what you learned about God as a "jealous" God. Discuss how this characteristic of God should affect believers' lives and interaction with the world. Use Colossians 3:5 and 1 John 2:15-17 to support your answer.

---

[1] James Strong, *The Exhaustive Concordance of the Bible: Showing Every Word of the Text of the Common English Version of the Canonical Books, and Every Occurrence of Each Word in Regular Order.*, electronic ed. (Ontario: Woodside Bible Fellowship., 1996). H7067.

© *2008 Precept Ministries International*

1. Before you move on to Exodus 35, you need to catch a biblical glimpse of Moses' shining face. Read Exodus 34:29-35 again and mark *the skin of his* (Moses) *face shone* and *veil*.

2. Now read 2 Corinthians 3:7-18. The text is printed below. Mark the following as you read:

   a. the *Old Covenant* or the *Law* (Sometimes it is referred to as "the letter.") Mark it with two stone tablets like this: ⌒. The Law is also referred to as:

   1) the "ministry of _____" and 2) the "ministry of _____."

   b. *Moses*

   c. *glory*

   d. the *veil* (Mark *unveiled* the same way, but put a line through it like this \.)

2 CORINTHIANS 3:7-18

7   But if the ministry of death, in letters engraved on stones, came with glory, so that the sons of Israel could not look intently at the face of Moses because of the glory of his face, fading *as* it was,

8   how shall the ministry of the Spirit fail to be even more with glory?

9   For if the ministry of condemnation has glory, much more does the ministry of righteousness abound in glory.

10 For indeed what had glory, in this case has no glory on account of the glory that surpasses *it*

11 For if that which fades away *wa*s with glory, much more that which remains *is* in glory.

12 Having therefore such a hope, we use great boldness in *our* speech,

13 and *are* not as Moses, *who* used to put a veil over his face that the sons of Israel might not look intently at the end of what was fading away.

14 But their minds were hardened; for until this very day at the reading of the old covenant the same veil remains unlifted, because it is removed in Christ.

15 But to this day whenever Moses is read, a veil lies over their heart;

16 but whenever a man turns to the Lord, the veil is taken away.

17 Now the Lord is the Spirit; and where the Spirit of the Lord is, *there* is liberty.

18 But we all, with unveiled face beholding as in a mirror the glory of the Lord, are being transformed into the same image from glory to glory, just as from the Lord, the Spirit.

© 2008 Precept Ministries International

3. This passage contains some difficult things to understand. Take it step by step and you will see an important and exciting truth!

   a. Start by listing what you learned about the Old Covenant. The first facts are listed for you.

      v. 7 – ministry of death
      – in letters engraved on stone
      – came with glory

   b. How was this glory seen?

   c. What ministry's glory surpasses the glory of the Old Covenant?

   d. Where is the glory of this ministry seen? (Look at verse 18.)

   e. How is this possible?

   f. Now, put these facts together. When Moses came down from the mountain after being with God and receiving His commands, the glory of the Lord shone on His face. It was evident to everyone that He had been with God. Is it evident to others that the Holy Spirit lives inside you? Can people look at your life and see the glory of God? If so, how? If not, why not?

          © 2008 Precept Ministries International

LESSON FOUR

1. Read Exodus 35-36:7. You will see the key repeated phrase *that the Lord has commanded* again.

   a. Mark the text using your key word bookmark including references to the *Lord's contribution* and to the *heart*.

   b. When you finish your observations, list below what you learned about the Lord's contribution and the heart. Watch for the *who*, *what*, *when*, *where*, *why*, and *how*.

THE LORD'S CONTRIBUTION	THE HEART

© 2008 Precept Ministries International

2. Examine your list. What have you learned that you can apply to your life and share with others?

3.   Record themes for Exodus 34-35 on the "At A Glance" chart.

How has God blessed you? Maybe He gifted you with unique talents. Maybe He blessed you with money or possessions. If He asked you to use those gifts and talents or to give back what He has given, would you be willing? Would you do it grudgingly or with a willing heart?

Consider this... how did Christ give to us? How much greater is what gave than what God asks from us?

                                                    © 2008 Precept Ministries International

LESSON FIVE

1. Your assignment today is simple. Read Exodus 36:8- 39:43 and mark the text.

    a. Mark the phrase *that the Lord had commanded*.

  b. As you read these chapters, you will find the material very repetitious (you already read the instructions about the furniture for the tabernacle in Exodus 25-30). Overall, only the verb tenses are different. In Exodus 25-30, the verbs are future. Now you will see *he made* repeated. Mark this and *what was made*.

    2. Record themes for Exodus 36-39 on the "At A Glance" chart.

© *2008 Precept Ministries International*

© 2008 Precept Ministries International

LESSON SIX

You're in the homestretch! Aren't you amazed at the task you're completing? You have read, marked, and studied all but one chapter in Exodus and now you will finish the book in this final lesson.

1. Read Exodus 40. It's an awesome picture you'll want to capture in your mind's eye. When you come to Exodus 40:34-38, stand in awe. Hear the "Hallelujah Chorus" in your heart as you think about God's glory filling the tabernacle. Also, be sure to mark key words from your bookmark including the following:

   a. *tabernacle*

   b. *cloud* and its synonyms

   c. *anointing* and the *oil*

   d. *consecrate*

   e. each piece of furniture

   f. time phrases

2. At the end of this lesson you will find a drawing of the tabernacle without the furniture. It's your task to place the furniture in it according to God's instructions to Moses. You can sketch or write them in their appropriate places – whichever will help you remember.

3. What did Moses, Aaron, and his sons do before entering the tent of meeting?

   a. Look up the following verses and list what you learn from them.

EXODUS 30:17-21

PSALM 24:1-6

PSALM 18:20-24

JOHN 13:5-10

b. How do these verses apply to you? What will achieve the blessings and righteousness of God?

© *2008 Precept Ministries International*

4. According to Exodus 40:17, when was the tabernacle built?

5. Record a theme for Exodus 40 on your "At A Glance" chart.

THE TABERNACLE

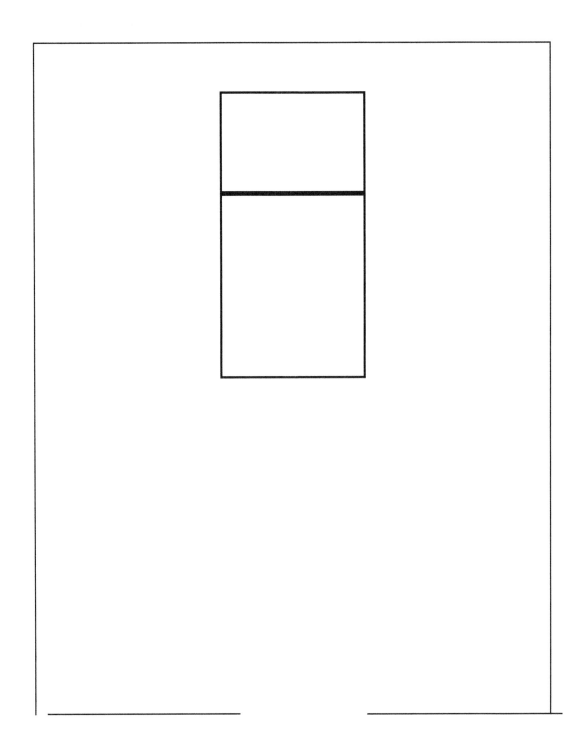

© *2008 Precept Ministries International*

THE FEASTS OF ISRAEL

Slaves in Egypt	1st Month (Nisan) — Festival of Passover				3rd Month (Sivan) — Festival of Pentecost
	Passover	Unleavened Bread	Firstfruits		Pentecost or Feast of Weeks
	Kill lamb & put blood on doorpost Exodus 12:6, 7	*Purging of all leaven* (symbol of sin)	*Wave offering of sheaf* (promise of harvest to come)		*Wave offering of two loaves of leavened bread*
	1st month, 14th day Leviticus 23:5	1st month, 15th day for 7 days Leviticus 23:6-8	Day after Sabbath Leviticus 23:9-14		50 days after firstfruits Leviticus 23:15-21
Whosoever commits sin is the slave to sin	**Christ our Passover has been sacrificed**	**Clean out old leaven... just as you are in fact unleavened**	**Christ has been raised...the firstfruits**	**Going away so Comforter can come**	**Promise of the Spirit, mystery of church: Jews-Gentiles in one body**
				Mount of Olives	
John 8:34	1 Corinthians 5:7	1 Corinthians 5:7, 8	1 Corinthians 15:20-23	John 16:7 Acts 1:9-12	Acts 2:1-47 1 Corinthians 12:13 Ephesians 2:11-22

Months: Nisan – *March, April*   Sivan – *May, June*   Tishri – *September, October*

© *2008 Precept Ministries International*

THE FEASTS OF ISRAEL

	7th Month (Tishri) Festival of Tabernacles		
	Feast of Trumpets	**Day of Atonement**	**Feast of Booths or Tabernacles**	
Interlude between fesivals	*Trumpet blown — a holy convocation*	*Atonement shall be made to cleanse you* Leviticus 16:30	*Harvest celebration memorial of tabernacles in wilderness*	
	7th month, 1st day Leviticus 23:23-25	7th month, 10th day Leviticus 23:26-32	7th month, 15th day, for 7 days; 8th day, Holy Convocation Leviticus 23:33-44	
	Regathering of Israel in preparation for final day of atonement Jeremiah 32:37-41	**Israel will repent and look to Messiah in one day** Zechariah 3:9, 10; 12:10; 13:1; 14:9	**Families of the earth will come to Jerusalem to celebrate the Feast of Booths** Zechariah 14:16-19	**New heaven and new earth** **God tabernacles with men** Revelation 21:1-3
		Coming of Christ		
	Ezekiel 36:24	Ezekiel 36:25-27 Hebrews 9, 10 Romans 11:25-29	Ezekiel 36:28	

Israel had two harvests each year – spring and autumn

© *2008 Precept Ministries International*

ENRICHMENT WORDS:

Jealous – be zealous.

© 2008 Precept Ministries International

CONTENTS:

- EXODUS 1-40 OBSERVATION WORKSHEETS

- MAP

- EXODUS "AT A GLANCE" CHART

- MY JOURNAL ON GOD

- ABOUT PRECEPT MINISTRIES INTERNATIONAL

© 2008 Precept Ministries International

© *2008 Precept Ministries International*

EXODUS 1
Observation Worksheet

Chapter Theme _____

NOW these are the names of the sons of Israel who came to Egypt with Jacob; they came each one with his household:

2   Reuben, Simeon, Levi and Judah;

3   Issachar, Zebulun and Benjamin;

4   Dan and Naphtali, Gad and Asher.

5   All the persons who came from the loins of Jacob were seventy in number, but Joseph was *already* in Egypt.

6   Joseph died, and all his brothers and all that generation.

7   But the sons of Israel were fruitful and increased greatly, and multiplied, and became exceedingly mighty, so that the land was filled with them.

8   Now a new king arose over Egypt, who did not know Joseph.

9   He said to his people, "Behold, the people of the sons of Israel are more and mightier than we.

10   "Come, let us deal wisely with them, or else they will multiply and in the event of war, they will also join themselves to those who hate us, and fight against us and depart from the land."

11   So they appointed taskmasters over them to afflict them with hard labor. And they built for Pharaoh storage cities, Pithom and Raamses.

12   But the more they afflicted them, the more they multiplied and the more they spread out, so that they were in dread of the sons of Israel.

13   The Egyptians compelled the sons of Israel to labor rigorously;

14   and they made their lives bitter with hard labor in mortar and bricks and at all *kinds* of labor in the field, all their labors which they rigorously imposed on them.

15   Then the king of Egypt spoke to the Hebrew midwives, one of whom was named Shiphrah and the other was named Puah;

© 2008 Precept Ministries International

16 and he said, "When you are helping the Hebrew women to give birth and see *them* upon the birthstool, if it is a son, then you shall put him to death; but if it is a daughter, then she shall live."

17 But the midwives feared God, and did not do as the king of Egypt had commanded them, but let the boys live.

18 So the king of Egypt called for the midwives and said to them, "Why have you done this thing, and let the boys live?"

19 The midwives said to Pharaoh, "Because the Hebrew women are not as the Egyptian women; for they are vigorous and give birth before the midwife can get to them."

20 So God was good to the midwives, and the people multiplied, and became very mighty.

21 Because the midwives feared God, He established households for them.

22 Then Pharaoh commanded all his people, saying, "Every son who is born you are to cast into the Nile, and every daughter you are to keep alive."

© *2008 Precept Ministries International*

EXODUS 2
Observation Worksheet

Chapter Theme _____

NOW a man from the house of Levi went and married a daughter of Levi.

2   The woman conceived and bore a son; and when she saw that he was beautiful, she hid him for three months.

3   But when she could hide him no longer, she got him a wicker basket and covered it over with tar and pitch. Then she put the child into it and set *it* among the reeds by the bank of the Nile.

4   His sister stood at a distance to find out what would happen to him.

5   The daughter of Pharaoh came down to bathe at the Nile, with her maidens walking alongside the Nile; and she saw the basket among the reeds and sent her maid, and she brought it *to her.*

6   When she opened *it,* she saw the child, and behold, *the* boy was crying. And she had pity on him and said, "This is one of the Hebrews' children."

7   Then his sister said to Pharaoh's daughter, "Shall I go and call a nurse for you from the Hebrew women that she may nurse the child for you?"

8   Pharaoh's daughter said to her, "Go *ahead.*" So the girl went and called the child's mother.

9   Then Pharaoh's daughter said to her, "Take this child away and nurse him for me and I will give *you* your wages." So the woman took the child and nursed him.

10   The child grew, and she brought him to Pharaoh's daughter and he became her son. And she named him Moses, and said, "Because I drew him out of the water."

11   Now it came about in those days, when Moses had grown up, that he went out to his brethren and looked on their hard labors; and he saw an Egyptian beating a Hebrew, one of his brethren.

12   So he looked this way and that, and when he saw there was no one *around,* he struck down the Egyptian and hid him in the sand.

13   He went out the next day, and behold, two Hebrews were fighting with each other; and he said to the offender, "Why are you striking your companion?"

© 2008 Precept Ministries International

14   But he said, "Who made you a prince or a judge over us? Are you intending to kill me as you killed the Egyptian?" Then Moses was afraid and said, "Surely the matter has become known."

15   When Pharaoh heard of this matter, he tried to kill Moses. But Moses fled from the presence of Pharaoh and settled in the land of Midian, and he sat down by a well.

16   Now the priest of Midian had seven daughters; and they came to draw water and filled the troughs to water their father's flock.

17   Then the shepherds came and drove them away, but Moses stood up and helped them and watered their flock.

18   When they came to Reuel their father, he said, "Why have you come *back* so soon today?"

19   So they said, "An Egyptian delivered us from the hand of the shepherds, and what is more, he even drew the water for us and watered the flock."

20   He said to his daughters, "Where is he then? Why is it that you have left the man behind? Invite him to have something to eat."

21   Moses was willing to dwell with the man, and he gave his daughter Zipporah to Moses.

22   Then she gave birth to a son, and he named him Gershom, for he said, "I have been a sojourner in a foreign land."

23   Now it came about in *the course of* those many days that the king of Egypt died. And the sons of Israel sighed because of the bondage, and they cried out; and their cry for help because of *their* bondage rose up to God.

24   So God heard their groaning; and God remembered His covenant with Abraham, Isaac, and Jacob.

25   God saw the sons of Israel, and God took notice *of them.*

© *2008 Precept Ministries International*

EXODUS 3
Observation Worksheet

Chapter Theme _____

NOW Moses was pasturing the flock of Jethro his father-in-law, the priest of Midian; and he led the flock to the west side of the wilderness and came to Horeb, the mountain of God.

2   The angel of the LORD appeared to him in a blazing fire from the midst of a bush; and he looked, and behold, the bush was burning with fire, yet the bush was not consumed.

3   So Moses said, "I must turn aside now and see this marvelous sight, why the bush is not burned up."

4   When the LORD saw that he turned aside to look, God called to him from the midst of the bush and said, "Moses, Moses!" And he said, "Here I am."

5   Then He said, "Do not come near here; remove your sandals from your feet, for the place on which you are standing is holy ground."

6   He said also, "I am the God of your father, the God of Abraham, the God of Isaac, and the God of Jacob." Then Moses hid his face, for he was afraid to look at God.

7   The LORD said, "I have surely seen the affliction of My people who are in Egypt, and have given heed to their cry because of their taskmasters, for I am aware of their sufferings.

8   "So I have come down to deliver them from the power of the Egyptians, and to bring them up from that land to a good and spacious land, to a land flowing with milk and honey, to the place of the Canaanite and the Hittite and the Amorite and the Perizzite and the Hivite and the Jebusite.

9   "Now, behold, the cry of the sons of Israel has come to Me; furthermore, I have seen the oppression with which the Egyptians are oppressing them.

10   "Therefore, come now, and I will send you to Pharaoh, so that you may bring My people, the sons of Israel, out of Egypt."

11   But Moses said to God, "Who am I, that I should go to Pharaoh, and that I should bring the sons of Israel out of Egypt?"

12   And He said, "Certainly I will be with you, and this shall be the sign to you that it is I who have sent you: when you have brought the people out of Egypt, you

© 2008 Precept Ministries International

shall worship God at this mountain."

13   Then Moses said to God, "Behold, I am going to the sons of Israel, and I will say to them, 'The God of your fathers has sent me to you.' Now they may say to me, 'What is His name?' What shall I say to them?"

14   God said to Moses, "I AM WHO I AM"; and He said, "Thus you shall say to the sons of Israel, 'I AM has sent me to you.' "

15   God, furthermore, said to Moses, "Thus you shall say to the sons of Israel, 'The LORD, the God of your fathers, the God of Abraham, the God of Isaac, and the God of Jacob, has sent me to you.' This is My name forever, and this is My memorial-name to all generations.

16   "Go and gather the elders of Israel together and say to them, 'The LORD, the God of your fathers, the God of Abraham, Isaac and Jacob, has appeared to me, saying, "I am indeed concerned about you and what has been done to you in Egypt.

17   "So I said, I will bring you up out of the affliction of Egypt to the land of the Canaanite and the Hittite and the Amorite and the Perizzite and the Hivite and the Jebusite, to a land flowing with milk and honey."'

18   "They will pay heed to what you say; and you with the elders of Israel will come to the king of Egypt and you will say to him, 'The LORD, the God of the Hebrews, has met with us. So now, please, let us go a three days' journey into the wilderness, that we may sacrifice to the LORD our God.'

19   "But I know that the king of Egypt will not permit you to go, except under compulsion.

20   "So I will stretch out My hand and strike Egypt with all My miracles which I shall do in the midst of it; and after that he will let you go.

21   "I will grant this people favor in the sight of the Egyptians; and it shall be that when you go, you will not go empty-handed.

22   "But every woman shall ask of her neighbor and the woman who lives in her house, articles of silver and articles of gold, and clothing; and you will put them on your sons and daughters. Thus you will plunder the Egyptians."

© *2008 Precept Ministries International*

EXODUS 4
Observation Worksheet

Chapter Theme _____

THEN Moses said, "What if they will not believe me or listen to what I say? For they may say, 'The LORD has not appeared to you.' "

2   The LORD said to him, "What is that in your hand?" And he said, "A staff."

3   Then He said, "Throw it on the ground." So he threw it on the ground, and it became a serpent; and Moses fled from it.

4   But the Lord said to Moses, "Stretch out your hand and grasp it by its tail"—so he stretched out his hand and caught it, and it became a staff in his hand—

5   "that they may believe that the LORD, the God of their fathers, the God of Abraham, the God of Isaac, and the God of Jacob, has appeared to you."

6   The LORD furthermore said to him, "Now put your hand into your bosom." So he put his hand into his bosom, and when he took it out, behold, his hand was leprous like snow.

7   Then He said, "Put your hand into your bosom again." So he put his hand into his bosom again, and when he took it out of his bosom, behold, it was restored like *the rest of* his flesh.

8   "If they will not believe you or heed the witness of the first sign, they may believe the witness of the last sign.

9   "But if they will not believe even these two signs or heed what you say, then you shall take some water from the Nile and pour it on the dry ground; and the water which you take from the Nile will become blood on the dry ground."

10 Then Moses said to the LORD, "Please, Lord, I have never been eloquent, neither recently nor in time past, nor since You have spoken to Your servant; for I am slow of speech and slow of tongue."

11 The LORD said to him, "Who has made man's mouth? Or who makes *him* mute or deaf, or seeing or blind? Is it not I, the LORD?

12 "Now then go, and I, even I, will be with your mouth, and teach you what you are to say."

13 But he said, "Please, Lord, now send *the message* by whomever You will."

14 Then the anger of the LORD burned against Moses, and He said, "Is there not your brother Aaron the Levite? I know that he speaks fluently. And moreover, behold, he is coming out to meet you; when he sees you, he will be glad in his heart.

© 2008 Precept Ministries International

15 "You are to speak to him and put the words in his mouth; and I, even I, will be with your mouth and his mouth, and I will teach you what you are to do.

16 "Moreover, he shall speak for you to the people; and he will be as a mouth for you and you will be as God to him.

17 "You shall take in your hand this staff, with which you shall perform the signs."

18 Then Moses departed and returned to Jethro his father-in-law and said to him, "Please, let me go, that I may return to my brethren who are in Egypt, and see if they are still alive." And Jethro said to Moses, "Go in peace."

19 Now the LORD said to Moses in Midian, "Go back to Egypt, for all the men who were seeking your life are dead."

20 So Moses took his wife and his sons and mounted them on a donkey, and returned to the land of Egypt. Moses also took the staff of God in his hand.

21 The LORD said to Moses, "When you go back to Egypt see that you perform before Pharaoh all the wonders which I have put in your power; but I will harden his heart so that he will not let the people go.

22 "Then you shall say to Pharaoh, 'Thus says the LORD, "Israel is My son, My first-born.

23 "So I said to you, 'Let My son go that he may serve Me'; but you have refused to let him go. Behold, I will kill your son, your firstborn."'"

24 Now it came about at the lodging place on the way that the LORD met him and sought to put him to death.

25 Then Zipporah took a flint and cut off her son's foreskin and threw it at Moses' feet, and she said, "You are indeed a bridegroom of blood to me."

26 So He let him alone. At that time she said, "*You are* a bridegroom of blood"— because of the circumcision.

27 Now the LORD said to Aaron, "Go to meet Moses in the wilderness." So he went and met him at the mountain of God and kissed him.

28 Moses told Aaron all the words of the LORD with which He had sent him, and all the signs that He had commanded him *to do*.

     © 2008 Precept Ministries International

29   Then Moses and Aaron went and assembled all the elders of the sons of Israel;

30   and Aaron spoke all the words which the Lord had spoken to Moses. He then performed the signs in the sight of the people.

31   So the people believed; and when they heard that the Lord was concerned about the sons of Israel and that He had seen their affliction, then they bowed low and worshiped.

© 2008 Precept Ministries International

© 2008 Precept Ministries International

EXODUS 5
Observation Worksheet

Chapter Theme _____

AND afterward Moses and Aaron came and said to Pharaoh, "Thus says the LORD, the God of Israel, 'Let My people go that they may celebrate a feast to Me in the wilderness.' "

2   But Pharaoh said, "Who is the LORD that I should obey His voice to let Israel go? I do not know the LORD, and besides, I will not let Israel go."

3   Then they said, "The God of the Hebrews has met with us. Please, let us go a three days' journey into the wilderness that we may sacrifice to the LORD our God, otherwise He will fall upon us with pestilence or with the sword."

4   But the king of Egypt said to them, "Moses and Aaron, why do you draw the people away from their work ? Get *back* to your labors !"

5   Again Pharaoh said, "Look, the people of the land are now many, and you would have them cease from their labors!"

6   So the same day Pharaoh commanded the taskmasters over the people and their foremen, saying,

7   "You are no longer to give the people straw to make brick as previously; let them go and gather straw for themselves.

8   "But the quota of bricks which they were making previously, you shall impose on them; you are not to reduce any of it. Because they are lazy, therefore they cry out, 'Let us go and sacrifice to our God.'

9   "Let the labor be heavier on the men, and let them work at it so that they will pay no attention to false words."

10   So the taskmasters of the people and their foremen went out and spoke to the people, saying, "Thus says Pharaoh, 'I am not going to give you *any* straw.

11   'You go *and* get straw for yourselves wherever you can find *it*, but none of your labor will be reduced.' "

12   So the people scattered through all the land of Egypt to gather stubble for straw.

13   The taskmasters pressed them, saying, "Complete your work quota, *your* daily amount, just as when you had straw."

14 Moreover, the foremen of the sons of Israel, whom Pharaoh's taskmasters had set over them, were beaten and were asked, "Why have you not completed your required amount either yesterday or today in making brick as previously?"

15 Then the foremen of the sons of Israel came and cried out to Pharaoh, saying, "Why do you deal this way with your servants?

16 "There is no straw given to your servants, yet they keep saying to us, 'Make bricks!' And behold, your servants are being beaten; but it is the fault of your *own* people."

17 But he said, "You are lazy, *very* lazy; therefore you say, 'Let us go *and* sacrifice to the LORD.'

18 "So go now *and* work; for you will be given no straw, yet you must deliver the quota of bricks."

19 The foremen of the sons of Israel saw that they were in trouble because they were told, "You must not reduce *your* daily amount of bricks."

20 When they left Pharaoh's presence, they met Moses and Aaron as they were waiting for them.

21 They said to them, "May the LORD look upon you and judge *you,* for you have made us odious in Pharaoh's sight and in the sight of his servants, to put a sword in their hand to kill us."

22 Then Moses returned to the LORD and said, "O Lord, why have You brought harm to this people? Why did You ever send me?

23 "Ever since I came to Pharaoh to speak in Your name, he has done harm to this people, and You have not delivered Your people at all."

© 2008 Precept Ministries International

EXODUS 6
Observation Worksheet

Chapter Theme _____

THEN the LORD said to Moses, "Now you shall see what I will do to Pharaoh; for under compulsion he will let them go, and under compulsion he will drive them out of his land."

2   God spoke further to Moses and said to him, "I am the LORD;

3   and I appeared to Abraham, Isaac, and Jacob, as God Almighty, but *by* My name, LORD, I did not make Myself known to them.

4   "I also established My covenant with them, to give them the land of Canaan, the land in which they sojourned.

5   "Furthermore I have heard the groaning of the sons of Israel, because the Egyptians are holding them in bondage, and I have remembered My covenant.

6   "Say, therefore, to the sons of Israel, 'I am the LORD, and I will bring you out from under the burdens of the Egyptians, and I will deliver you from their bondage. I will also redeem you with an outstretched arm and with great judgments.

7   'Then I will take you for My people, and I will be your God; and you shall know that I am the LORD your God, who brought you out from under the burdens of the Egyptians.

8   'I will bring you to the land which I swore to give to Abraham, Isaac, and Jacob, and I will give it to you *for* a possession; I am the LORD.' "

9   So Moses spoke thus to the sons of Israel, but they did not listen to Moses on account of *their* despondency and cruel bondage.

10   Now the LORD spoke to Moses, saying,

11   "Go, tell Pharaoh king of Egypt to let the sons of Israel go out of his land."

12   But Moses spoke before the LORD, saying, "Behold, the sons of Israel have not listened to me; how then will Pharaoh listen to me, for I am unskilled in speech?"

© 2008 Precept Ministries International

13   Then the Lord spoke to Moses and to Aaron, and gave them a charge to the sons of Israel and to Pharaoh king of Egypt, to bring the sons of Israel out of the land of Egypt.

14   These are the heads of their fathers' households. The sons of Reuben, Israel's firstborn: Hanoch and Pallu, Hezron and Carmi; these are the families of Reuben.

15   The sons of Simeon: Jemuel and Jamin and Ohad and Jachin and Zohar and Shaul the son of a Canaanite woman; these are the families of Simeon.

16   These are the names of the sons of Levi according to their generations: Gershon and Kohath and Merari; and the length of Levi's life was one hundred and thirty-seven years.

17   The sons of Gershon: Libni and Shimei, according to their families.

18   The sons of Kohath: Amram and Izhar and Hebron and Uzziel; and the length of Kohath's life was one hundred and thirty-three years.

19   The sons of Merari: Mahli and Mushi. These are the families of the Levites according to their generations.

20   Amram married his father's sister Jochebed, and she bore him Aaron and Moses; and the length of Amram's life was one hundred and thirty-seven years.

21   The sons of Izhar: Korah and Nepheg and Zichri.

22   The sons of Uzziel: Mishael and Elzaphan and Sithri.

23   Aaron married Elisheba, the daughter of Amminadab, the sister of Nahshon, and she bore him Nadab and Abihu, Eleazar and Ithamar.

24   The sons of Korah: Assir and Elkanah and Abiasaph ; these are the families of the Korahites.

25   Aaron's son Eleazar married one of the daughters of Putiel, and she bore him Phinehas. These are the heads of the fathers' *households* of the Levites according to their families.

26   It was *the same* Aaron and Moses to whom the Lord said, "Bring out the sons of Israel from the land of Egypt according to their hosts."

                                             © *2008 Precept Ministries International*

27 They were the ones who spoke to Pharaoh king of Egypt about bringing out the sons of Israel from Egypt; it was *the same* Moses and Aaron.

28 Now it came about on the day when the Lᴏʀᴅ spoke to Moses in the land of Egypt,

29 that the Lᴏʀᴅ spoke to Moses, saying, "I am the Lᴏʀᴅ; speak to Pharaoh king of Egypt all that I speak to you."

30 But Moses said before the Lᴏʀᴅ, "Behold, I am unskilled in speech; how then will Pharaoh listen to me?"

© 2008 Precept Ministries International

EXODUS 7
Observation Worksheet

Chapter Theme _____

THEN the LORD said to Moses, "See, I make you *as* God to Pharaoh, and your brother Aaron shall be your prophet.

2   "You shall speak all that I command you, and your brother Aaron shall speak to Pharaoh that he let the sons of Israel go out of his land.

3   "But I will harden Pharaoh's heart that I may multiply My signs and My wonders in the land of Egypt.

4   "When Pharaoh does not listen to you, then I will lay My hand on Egypt and bring out My hosts, My people the sons of Israel, from the land of Egypt by great judgments.

5   "The Egyptians shall know that I am the LORD, when I stretch out My hand on Egypt and bring out the sons of Israel from their midst."

6   So Moses and Aaron did *it;* as the LORD commanded them, thus they did.

7   Moses was eighty years old and Aaron eighty -three, when they spoke to Pharaoh.

8   Now the LORD spoke to Moses and Aaron, saying,

9   "When Pharaoh speaks to you, saying, 'Work a miracle,' then you shall say to Aaron, 'Take your staff and throw *it* down before Pharaoh, *that* it may become a serpent.' "

10   So Moses and Aaron came to Pharaoh, and thus they did just as the LORD had commanded; and Aaron threw his staff down before Pharaoh and his servants, and it became a serpent.

11   Then Pharaoh also called for *the* wise men and *the* sorcerers, and they also, the magicians of Egypt, did the same with their secret arts.

12   For each one threw down his staff and they turned into serpents. But Aaron's staff swallowed up their staffs.

© 2008 Precept Ministries International

13   Yet Pharaoh's heart was hardened, and he did not listen to them, as the LORD had said.

14   Then the LORD said to Moses, "Pharaoh's heart is stubborn ; he refuses to let the people go.

15   "Go to Pharaoh in the morning as he is going out to the water, and station yourself to meet him on the bank of the Nile; and you shall take in your hand the staff that was turned into a serpent.

16   "You shall say to him, 'The LORD, the God of the Hebrews, sent me to you, saying, "Let My people go, that they may serve Me in the wilderness. But behold, you have not listened until now."

17   'Thus says the LORD, "By this you shall know that I am the LORD: behold, I will strike the water that is in the Nile with the staff that is in my hand, and it will be turned to blood.

18   "The fish that are in the Nile will die, and the Nile will become foul, and the Egyptians will find difficulty in drinking water from the Nile."'"

19   Then the LORD said to Moses, "Say to Aaron, 'Take your staff and stretch out your hand over the waters of Egypt, over their rivers, over their streams, and over their pools, and over all their reservoirs of water, that they may become blood; and there will be blood throughout all the land of Egypt, both in *vessels of* wood and in *vessels of* stone.'"

20   So Moses and Aaron did even as the LORD had commanded. And he lifted up the staff and struck the water that *was* in the Nile, in the sight of Pharaoh and in the sight of his servants, and all the water that *was* in the Nile was turned to blood.

21   The fish that *were* in the Nile died, and the Nile became foul, so that the Egyptians could not drink water from the Nile. And the blood was through all the land of Egypt.

22   But the magicians of Egypt did the same with their secret arts; and Pharaoh's heart was hardened, and he did not listen to them, as the LORD had said.

23   Then Pharaoh turned and went into his house with no concern even for this.

24   So all the Egyptians dug around the Nile for water to drink, for they could not drink of the water of the Nile.

25   Seven days passed after the Lord had struck the Nile.

© 2008 Precept Ministries International

EXODUS 8
Observation Worksheet

Chapter Theme _____

THEN the Lord said to Moses, "Go to Pharaoh and say to him, 'Thus says the Lord, "Let My people go, that they may serve Me.

2   "But if you refuse to let *them* go, behold, I will smite your whole territory with frogs.

3   "The Nile will swarm with frogs, which will come up and go into your house and into your bedroom and on your bed, and into the houses of your servants and on your people, and into your ovens and into your kneading bowls.

4   "So the frogs will come up on you and your people and all your servants."'"

5   Then the Lord said to Moses, "Say to Aaron, 'Stretch out your hand with your staff over the rivers, over the streams and over the pools, and make frogs come up on the land of Egypt.' "

6   So Aaron stretched out his hand over the waters of Egypt, and the frogs came up and covered the land of Egypt.

7   The magicians did the same with their secret arts, making frogs come up on the land of Egypt.

8   Then Pharaoh called for Moses and Aaron and said, "Entreat the Lord that He remove the frogs from me and from my people; and I will let the people go, that they may sacrifice to the Lord."

9   Moses said to Pharaoh, "The honor is yours to tell me: when shall I entreat for you and your servants and your people, that the frogs be destroyed from you and your houses, *that* they may be left only in the Nile?"

10   Then he said, "Tomorrow." So he said, "*May it be* according to your word, that you may know that there is no one like the Lord our God.

11   "The frogs will depart from you and your houses and your servants and your people; they will be left only in the Nile."

© 2008 Precept Ministries International

12 Then Moses and Aaron went out from Pharaoh, and Moses cried to the LORD concerning the frogs which He had inflicted upon Pharaoh.

13 The LORD did according to the word of Moses, and the frogs died out of the houses, the courts, and the fields.

14 So they piled them in heaps, and the land became foul.

15 But when Pharaoh saw that there was relief, he hardened his heart and did not listen to them, as the LORD had said.

16 Then the LORD said to Moses, "Say to Aaron, 'Stretch out your staff and strike the dust of the earth, that it may become gnats through all the land of Egypt.' "

17 They did so; and Aaron stretched out his hand with his staff, and struck the dust of the earth, and there were gnats on man and beast. All the dust of the earth became gnats through all the land of Egypt.

18 The magicians tried with their secret arts to bring forth gnats, but they could not; so there were gnats on man and beast.

19 Then the magicians said to Pharaoh, "This is the finger of God." But Pharaoh's heart was hardened, and he did not listen to them, as the LORD had said.

20 Now the LORD said to Moses, "Rise early in the morning and present yourself before Pharaoh, as he comes out to the water, and say to him, 'Thus says the LORD, "Let My people go, that they may serve Me.

21 "For if you do not let My people go, behold, I will send swarms of flies on you and on your servants and on your people and into your houses; and the houses of the Egyptians will be full of swarms of flies, and also the ground on which they *dwell.*

22 "But on that day I will set apart the land of Goshen, where My people are living, so that no swarms of flies will be there, in order that you may know that I, the LORD, am in the midst of the land.

23 "I will put a division between My people and your people. Tomorrow this sign will occur." ' "

24 Then the LORD did so. And there came great swarms of flies into the house of Pharaoh and the houses of his servants and the land was laid waste because of

© *2008 Precept Ministries International*

the swarms of flies in all the land of Egypt.

25 Pharaoh called for Moses and Aaron and said, "Go, sacrifice to your God within the land."

26 But Moses said, "It is not right to do so, for we will sacrifice to the LORD our God what is an abomination to the Egyptians. If we sacrifice what is an abomination to the Egyptians before their eyes, will they not then stone us?

27 "We must go a three days' journey into the wilderness and sacrifice to the LORD our God as He commands us."

28 Pharaoh said, "I will let you go, that you may sacrifice to the LORD your God in the wilderness; only you shall not go very far away. Make supplication for me."

29 Then Moses said, "Behold, I am going out from you, and I shall make supplication to the LORD that the swarms of flies may depart from Pharaoh, from his servants, and from his people tomorrow; only do not let Pharaoh deal deceitfully again in not letting the people go to sacrifice to the LORD."

30 So Moses went out from Pharaoh and made supplication to the LORD.

31 The LORD did as Moses asked, and removed the swarms of flies from Pharaoh, from his servants and from his people; not one remained.

32 But Pharaoh hardened his heart this time also, and he did not let the people go.

© 2008 Precept Ministries International

© *2008 Precept Ministries International*

EXODUS 9
Observation Worksheet

Chapter Theme _____

THEN the Lord said to Moses, "Go to Pharaoh and speak to him, 'Thus says the Lord, the God of the Hebrews, "Let My people go, that they may serve Me.

2   "For if you refuse to let *them* go and continue to hold them,

3   behold, the hand of the Lord will come *with* a very severe pestilence on your livestock which are in the field, on the horses, on the donkeys, on the camels, on the herds, and on the flocks.

4   "But the Lord will make a distinction between the livestock of Israel and the livestock of Egypt, so that nothing will die of all that belongs to the sons of Israel."'"

5   The Lord set a definite time, saying, "Tomorrow the Lord will do this thing in the land."

6   So the Lord did this thing on the next day, and all the livestock of Egypt died; but of the livestock of the sons of Israel, not one died.

7   Pharaoh sent, and behold, there was not even one of the livestock of Israel dead. But the heart of Pharaoh was hardened, and he did not let the people go.

8   Then the Lord said to Moses and Aaron, "Take for yourselves handfuls of soot from a kiln, and let Moses throw it toward the sky in the sight of Pharaoh.

9   "It will become fine dust over all the land of Egypt, and will become boils breaking out with sores on man and beast through all the land of Egypt."

10   So they took soot from a kiln, and stood before Pharaoh; and Moses threw it toward the sky, and it became boils breaking out with sores on man and beast.

11   The magicians could not stand before Moses because of the boils, for the boils were on the magicians as well as on all the Egyptians.

12   And the Lord hardened Pharaoh's heart, and he did not listen to them, just as the Lord had spoken to Moses.

13   Then the Lord said to Moses, "Rise up early in the morning and stand before Pharaoh and say to him, 'Thus says the Lord, the God of the Hebrews, "Let My people go, that they may serve Me.

14   "For this time I will send all My plagues on you and your servants and your people, so that you may know that there is no one like Me in all the earth.

15   "For *if by* now I had put forth My hand and struck you and your people with pestilence, you would then have been cut off from the earth.

16   "But, indeed, for this reason I have allowed you to remain, in order to show you My power and in order to proclaim My name through all the earth.

17   "Still you exalt yourself against My people by not letting them go.

© *2008 Precept Ministries International*

18 "Behold, about this time tomorrow, I will send a very heavy hail, such as has not been *seen* in Egypt from the day it was founded until now.

19 "Now therefore send, bring your livestock and whatever you have in the field to safety. Every man and beast that is found in the field and is not brought home, when the hail comes down on them, will die."'"

20 The one among the servants of Pharaoh who feared the word of the LORD made his servants and his livestock flee into the houses;

21 but he who paid no regard to the word of the LORD left his servants and his livestock in the field.

22 Now the LORD said to Moses, "Stretch out your hand toward the sky, that hail may fall on all the land of Egypt, on man and on beast and on every plant of the field, throughout the land of Egypt."

23 Moses stretched out his staff toward the sky, and the Lord sent thunder and hail, and fire ran down to the earth. And the Lord rained hail on the land of Egypt.

24 So there was hail, and fire flashing continually in the midst of the hail, very severe, such as had not been in all the land of Egypt since it became a nation.

25 The hail struck all that was in the field through all the land of Egypt, both man and beast; the hail also struck every plant of the field and shattered every tree of the field.

26 Only in the land of Goshen, where the sons of Israel *were,* there was no hail.

27 Then Pharaoh sent for Moses and Aaron, and said to them, "I have sinned this time; the LORD is the righteous one, and I and my people are the wicked ones.

28 "Make supplication to the LORD, for there has been enough of God's thunder and hail; and I will let you go, and you shall stay no longer."

29 Moses said to him, "As soon as I go out of the city, I will spread out my hands to the LORD; the thunder will cease and there will be hail no longer, that you may know that the earth is the LORD's.

30 "But as for you and your servants, I know that you do not yet fear the LORD God."

31 (Now the flax and the barley were ruined, for the barley was in the ear and the flax was in bud.

32 But the wheat and the spelt were not ruined, for they *ripen* late.)

33 So Moses went out of the city from Pharaoh, and spread out his hands to the LORD; and the thunder and the hail ceased, and rain no longer poured on the earth.

34 But when Pharaoh saw that the rain and the hail and the thunder had ceased, he sinned again and hardened his heart, he and his servants.

35 Pharaoh's heart was hardened, and he did not let the sons of Israel go, just as the LORD had spoken through Moses.

© *2008 Precept Ministries International*

EXODUS 10
Observation Worksheet

Chapter Theme _____

THEN the Lord said to Moses, "Go to Pharaoh, for I have hardened his heart and the heart of his servants, that I may perform these signs of Mine among them,

2   and that you may tell in the hearing of your son, and of your grandson, how I made a mockery of the Egyptians and how I performed My signs among them, that you may know that I am the LORD."

3   Moses and Aaron went to Pharaoh and said to him, "Thus says the LORD, the God of the Hebrews, 'How long will you refuse to humble yourself before Me? Let My people go, that they may serve Me.

4   'For if you refuse to let My people go, behold, tomorrow I will bring locusts into your territory.

5   'They shall cover the surface of the land, so that no one will be able to see the land. They will also eat the rest of what has escaped—what is left to you from the hail—and they will eat every tree which sprouts for you out of the field.

6   'Then your houses shall be filled and the houses of all your servants and the houses of all the Egyptians, something which neither your fathers nor your grandfathers have seen, from the day that they came upon the earth until this day.' "And he turned and went out from Pharaoh.

7   Pharaoh's servants said to him, "How long will this man be a snare to us? Let the men go, that they may serve the LORD their God. Do you not realize that Egypt is destroyed?"

8   So Moses and Aaron were brought back to Pharaoh, and he said to them, "Go, serve the Lord your God! Who are the ones that are going?"

9   Moses said, "We shall go with our young and our old; with our sons and our daughters, with our flocks and our herds we shall go, for we must hold a feast to the LORD."

10   Then he said to them, "Thus may the LORD be with you, if ever I let you and

your little ones go! Take heed, for evil is in your mind.

11 "Not so! Go now, the men among you, and serve the Lord, for that is what you desire." So they were driven out from Pharaoh's presence.

12 Then the Lord said to Moses, "Stretch out your hand over the land of Egypt for the locusts, that they may come up on the land of Egypt and eat every plant of the land, even all that the hail has left."

13 So Moses stretched out his staff over the land of Egypt, and the Lord directed an east wind on the land all that day and all that night; and when it was morning, the east wind brought the locusts.

14 The locusts came up over all the land of Egypt and settled in all the territory of Egypt; they were very numerous. There had never been so many locusts, nor would there be so many again.

15 For they covered the surface of the whole land, so that the land was darkened; and they ate every plant of the land and all the fruit of the trees that the hail had left. Thus nothing green was left on tree or plant of the field through all the land of Egypt.

16 Then Pharaoh hurriedly called for Moses and Aaron, and he said, "I have sinned against the Lord your God and against you.

17 "Now therefore, please forgive my sin only this once, and make supplication to the Lord your God, that He would only remove this death from me."

18 He went out from Pharaoh and made supplication to the Lord.

19 So the Lord shifted the wind to a very strong west wind which took up the locusts and drove them into the Red Sea; not one locust was left in all the territory of Egypt.

20 But the Lord hardened Pharaoh's heart, and he did not let the sons of Israel go.

21 Then the Lord said to Moses, "Stretch out your hand toward the sky, that there may be darkness over the land of Egypt, even a darkness which may be felt."

22 So Moses stretched out his hand toward the sky, and there was thick darkness in all the land of Egypt for three days.

23 They did not see one another, nor did anyone rise from his place for three days,

© *2008 Precept Ministries International*

but all the sons of Israel had light in their dwellings.

24 Then Pharaoh called to Moses, and said, "Go, serve the LORD; only let your flocks and your herds be detained. Even your little ones may go with you."

25 But Moses said, "You must also let us have sacrifices and burnt offerings, that we may sacrifice them to the LORD our God.

26 "Therefore, our livestock too shall go with us; not a hoof shall be left behind, for we shall take some of them to serve the LORD our God. And until we arrive there, we ourselves do not know with what we shall serve the LORD."

27 But the Lord hardened Pharaoh's heart, and he was not willing to let them go.

28 Then Pharaoh said to him, "Get away from me! Beware, do not see my face again, for in the day you see my face you shall die!"

29 Moses said, "You are right; I shall never see your face again!"

© 2008 Precept Ministries International

Exodus
Exodus 10

© *2008 Precept Ministries International*

EXODUS 11
Observation Worksheet

Chapter Theme _____

NOW the LORD said to Moses, "One more plague I will bring on Pharaoh and on Egypt; after that he will let you go from here. When he lets you go, he will surely drive you out from here completely.

2   "Speak now in the hearing of the people that each man ask from his neighbor and each woman from her neighbor for articles of silver and articles of gold."

3   The LORD gave the people favor in the sight of the Egyptians. Furthermore, the man Moses *himself* was greatly esteemed in the land of Egypt, *both* in the sight of Pharaoh's servants and in the sight of the people.

4   Moses said, "Thus says the LORD, 'About midnight I am going out into the midst of Egypt,

5   and all the firstborn in the land of Egypt shall die, from the firstborn of the Pharaoh who sits on his throne, even to the firstborn of the slave girl who is behind the millstones; all the firstborn of the cattle as well.

6   'Moreover, there shall be a great cry in all the land of Egypt, such as there has not been *before* and such as shall never be again.

7   'But against any of the sons of Israel a dog will not *even* bark, whether against man or beast, that you may understand how the LORD makes a distinction between Egypt and Israel.'

8   "All these your servants will come down to me and bow themselves before me, saying, 'Go out, you and all the people who follow you,' and after that I will go out." And he went out from Pharaoh in hot anger.

9   Then the LORD said to Moses, "Pharaoh will not listen to you, so that My wonders will be multiplied in the land of Egypt."

10 Moses and Aaron performed all these wonders before Pharaoh; yet the LORD hardened Pharaoh's heart, and he did not let the sons of Israel go out of his land.

© 2008 Precept Ministries International

Exodus
Exodus 11

© *2008 Precept Ministries International*

EXODUS 12
Observation Worksheet

Chapter Theme _____

NOW the LORD said to Moses and Aaron in the land of Egypt,

2   "This month shall be the beginning of months for you; it is to be the first month of the year to you.

3   "Speak to all the congregation of Israel, saying, 'On the tenth of this month they are each one to take a lamb for themselves, according to their fathers' households, a lamb for each household.

4   'Now if the household is too small for a lamb, then he and his neighbor nearest to his house are to take one according to the number of persons *in them;* according to what each man should eat, you are to divide the lamb.

5   'Your lamb shall be an unblemished male a year old; you may take it from the sheep or from the goats.

6   'You shall keep it until the fourteenth day of the same month, then the whole assembly of the congregation of Israel is to kill it at twilight.

7   'Moreover, they shall take some of the blood and put it on the two doorposts and on the lintel of the houses in which they eat it.

8   'They shall eat the flesh that *same* night, roasted with fire, and they shall eat it with unleavened bread and bitter herbs.

9   'Do not eat any of it raw or boiled at all with water, but rather roasted with fire, *both* its head and its legs along with its entrails.

10 'And you shall not leave any of it over until morning, but whatever is left of it until morning, you shall burn with fire.

11 'Now you shall eat it in this manner: *with* your loins girded, your sandals on your feet, and your staff in your hand; and you shall eat it in haste—it is the LORD'S Passover.

12 'For I will go through the land of Egypt on that night, and will strike down all the firstborn in the land of Egypt, both man and beast; and against all the gods of Egypt I will execute judgments—I am the LORD.

13 'The blood shall be a sign for you on the houses where you live ; and when I

© *2008 Precept Ministries International*

see the blood I will pass over you, and no plague will befall you to destroy *you* when I strike the land of Egypt.

14 'Now this day will be a memorial to you, and you shall celebrate it *as* a feast to the LORD; throughout your generations you are to celebrate it *as* a permanent ordinance.

15 'Seven days you shall eat unleavened bread, but on the first day you shall remove leaven from your houses; for whoever eats anything leavened from the first day until the seventh day, that person shall be cut off from Israel.

16 'On the first day you shall have a holy assembly, and *another* holy assembly on the seventh day; no work at all shall be done on them, except what must be eaten by every person, that alone may be prepared by you.

17 'You shall also observe the *Feast of* Unleavened Bread, for on this very day I brought your hosts out of the land of Egypt; therefore you shall observe this day throughout your generations as a permanent ordinance.

18 'In the first *month,* on the fourteenth day of the month at evening, you shall eat unleavened bread, until the twenty-first day of the month at evening.

19 'Seven days there shall be no leaven found in your houses; for whoever eats what is leavened, that person shall be cut off from the congregation of Israel, whether *he is* an alien or a native of the land.

20 'You shall not eat anything leavened; in all your dwellings you shall eat unleavened bread.' "

21 Then Moses called for all the elders of Israel and said to them, "Go and take for yourselves lambs according to your families, and slay the Passover *lamb.*

22 "You shall take a bunch of hyssop and dip it in the blood which is in the basin, and apply some of the blood that is in the basin to the lintel and the two doorposts; and none of you shall go outside the door of his house until morning.

23 "For the LORD will pass through to smite the Egyptians; and when He sees the blood on the lintel and on the two doorposts, the LORD will pass over the door

© *2008 Precept Ministries International*

and will not allow the destroyer to come in to your houses to smite *you.*

24 "And you shall observe this event as an ordinance for you and your children for-ever.

25 "When you enter the land which the LORD will give you, as He has promised, you shall observe this rite.

26 "And when your children say to you, 'What does this rite mean to you?'

27 you shall say, 'It is a Passover sacrifice to the LORD who passed over the houses of the sons of Israel in Egypt when He smote the Egyptians, but spared our homes.' " And the people bowed low and worshiped.

28 Then the sons of Israel went and did *so;* just as the LORD had commanded Moses and Aaron, so they did.

29 Now it came about at midnight that the LORD struck all the firstborn in the land of Egypt, from the firstborn of Pharaoh who sat on his throne to the firstborn of the captive who was in the dungeon, and all the firstborn of cattle.

30 Pharaoh arose in the night, he and all his servants and all the Egyptians, and there was a great cry in Egypt, for there was no home where there was not someone dead.

31 Then he called for Moses and Aaron at night and said, "Rise up, get out from among my people, both you and the sons of Israel; and go, worship the LORD, as you have said.

32 "Take both your flocks and your herds, as you have said, and go, and bless me also."

33 The Egyptians urged the people, to send them out of the land in haste, for they said, "We will all be dead."

34 So the people took their dough before it was leavened, *with* their kneading bowls bound up in the clothes on their shoulders.

35 Now the sons of Israel had done according to the word of Moses, for they had requested from the Egyptians articles of silver and articles of gold, and cloth-ing;

© 2008 Precept Ministries International

36   and the LORD had given the people favor in the sight of the Egyptians, so that they let them have their request. Thus they plundered the Egyptians.

37   Now the sons of Israel journeyed from Rameses to Succoth, about six hundred thousand men on foot, aside from children.

38   A mixed multitude also went up with them, along with flocks and herds, a very large number of livestock.

39   They baked the dough which they had brought out of Egypt into cakes of unleavened bread. For it had not become leavened, since they were driven out of Egypt and could not delay, nor had they prepared any provisions for themselves.

40   Now the time that the sons of Israel lived in Egypt was four hundred and thirty years.

41   And at the end of four hundred and thirty years, to the very day, all the hosts of the LORD went out from the land of Egypt.

42   It is a night to be observed for the LORD for having brought them out from the land of Egypt; this night is for the LORD, to be observed by all the sons of Israel throughout their generations.

43   The LORD said to Moses and Aaron, "This is the ordinance of the Passover: no foreigner is to eat of it;

44   but every man's slave purchased with money, after you have circumcised him, then he may eat of it.

45   "A sojourner or a hired servant shall not eat of it.

46   "It is to be eaten in a single house; you are not to bring forth any of the flesh outside of the house, nor are you to break any bone of it.

47   "All the congregation of Israel are to celebrate this.

48   "But if a stranger sojourns with you, and celebrates the Passover to the LORD, let all his males be circumcised, and then let him come near to celebrate it; and he shall be like a native of the land. But no uncircumcised person may eat of it.

49   "The same law shall apply to the native as to the stranger who sojourns among you."

                                                                                  © *2008 Precept Ministries International*

50 Then all the sons of Israel did *so;* they did just as the Lord had commanded Moses and Aaron.

51 And on that same day the Lord brought the sons of Israel out of the land of Egypt by their hosts.

© *2008 Precept Ministries International*

EXODUS 13
Observation Worksheet

Chapter Theme _____

THEN the LORD spoke to Moses, saying,

2   "Sanctify to Me every firstborn, the first offspring of every womb among the sons of Israel, both of man and beast; it belongs to Me."

3   Moses said to the people, "Remember this day in which you went out from Egypt, from the house of slavery ; for by a powerful hand the LORD brought you out from this place. And nothing leavened shall be eaten.

4   "On this day in the month of Abib, you are about to go forth.

5   "It shall be when the LORD brings you to the land of the Canaanite, the Hittite, the Amorite, the Hivite and the Jebusite, which He swore to your fathers to give you, a land flowing with milk and honey, that you shall observe this rite in this month.

6   "For seven days you shall eat unleavened bread, and on the seventh day there shall be a feast to the LORD.

7   "Unleavened bread shall be eaten throughout the seven days; and nothing leavened shall be seen among you, nor shall any leaven be seen among you in all your borders.

8   "You shall tell your son on that day, saying, 'It is because of what the LORD did for me when I came out of Egypt.'

9   "And it shall serve as a sign to you on your hand, and as a reminder on your forehead, that the law of the LORD may be in your mouth; for with a powerful hand the LORD brought you out of Egypt.

10   "Therefore, you shall keep this ordinance at its appointed time from year to year.

11   "Now when the LORD brings you to the land of the Canaanite, as He swore to you and to your fathers, and gives it to you,

12   you shall devote to the Lord the first offspring of every womb, and the first offspring of

© 2008 Precept Ministries International

every beast that you own; the males belong to the LORD.

13 "But every first offspring of a donkey you shall redeem with a lamb, but if you do not redeem *it,* then you shall break its neck; and every firstborn of man among your sons you shall redeem.

14 "And it shall be when your son asks you in time to come, saying, 'What is this?' then you shall say to him, 'With a powerful hand the LORD brought us out of Egypt, from the house of slavery.

15 'It came about, when Pharaoh was stubborn about letting us go, that the LORD killed every firstborn in the land of Egypt, both the firstborn of man and the firstborn of beast. Therefore, I sacrifice to the LORD the males, the first offspring of every womb, but every firstborn of my sons I redeem.'

16 "So it shall serve as a sign on your hand and as phylacteries on your forehead, for with a powerful hand the LORD brought us out of Egypt."

17 Now when Pharaoh had let the people go, God did not lead them by the way of the land of the Philistines, even though it was near; for God said, "The people might change their minds when they see war, and return to Egypt."

18 Hence God led the people around by the way of the wilderness to the Red Sea; and the sons of Israel went up in martial array from the land of Egypt.

19 Moses took the bones of Joseph with him, for he had made the sons of Israel solemnly swear, saying, "God will surely take care of you, and you shall carry my bones from here with you."

20 Then they set out from Succoth and camped in Etham on the edge of the wilderness.

21 The LORD was going before them in a pillar of cloud by day to lead them on the way, and in a pillar of fire by night to give them light, that they might travel by day and by night.

22 He did not take away the pillar of cloud by day, nor the pillar of fire by night, from before the people.

© 2008 Precept Ministries International

© 2008 Precept Ministries International

EXODUS 14
Observation Worksheet

Chapter Theme _____

NOW the LORD spoke to Moses, saying,

2   "Tell the sons of Israel to turn back and camp before Pi-hahiroth, between Migdol and the sea; you shall camp in front of Baal-zephon, opposite it, by the sea.

3   "For Pharaoh will say of the sons of Israel, 'They are wandering aimlessly in the land; the wilderness has shut them in.'

4   "Thus I will harden Pharaoh's heart, and he will chase after them; and I will be honored through Pharaoh and all his army, and the Egyptians will know that I am the LORD." And they did so.

5   When the king of Egypt was told that the people had fled, Pharaoh and his servants had a change of heart toward the people, and they said, "What is this we have done, that we have let Israel go from serving us?"

6   So he made his chariot ready and took his people with him;

7   and he took six hundred select chariots, and all the *other* chariots of Egypt with officers over all of them.

8   The LORD hardened the heart of Pharaoh, king of Egypt, and he chased after the sons of Israel as the sons of Israel were going out boldly.

9   Then the Egyptians chased after them *with* all the horses *and* chariots of Pharaoh, his horsemen and his army, and they overtook them camping by the sea, beside Pi-hahiroth, in front of Baal-zephon.

10   As Pharaoh drew near, the sons of Israel looked, and behold, the Egyptians were marching after them, and they became very frightened; so the sons of Israel cried out to the LORD.

11   Then they said to Moses, "Is it because there were no graves in Egypt that you have taken us away to die in the wilderness? Why have you dealt with us in this way, bringing us out of Egypt?

12   "Is this not the word that we spoke to you in Egypt, saying, 'Leave us alone that we may serve the Egyptians'? For it would have been better for us to serve the Egyptians than to die in the wilderness."

13   But Moses said to the people, "Do not fear! Stand by and see the salvation of the LORD which He will accomplish for you today; for the Egyptians whom you have seen today, you will never see them again forever.

14   "The LORD will fight for you while you keep silent."

15   Then the LORD said to Moses, "Why are you crying out to Me? Tell the sons of Israel to go forward.

Exodus
Exodus 14

16 "As for you, lift up your staff and stretch out your hand over the sea and divide it, and the sons of Israel shall go through the midst of the sea on dry land.

17 "As for Me, behold, I will harden the hearts of the Egyptians so that they will go in after them; and I will be honored through Pharaoh and all his army, through his chariots and his horsemen.

18 "Then the Egyptians will know that I am the LORD, when I am honored through Pharaoh, through his chariots and his horsemen."

19 The angel of God, who had been going before the camp of Israel, moved and went behind them; and the pillar of cloud moved from before them and stood behind them.

20 So it came between the camp of Egypt and the camp of Israel; and there was the cloud along with the darkness, yet it gave light at night. Thus the one did not come near the other all night.

21 Then Moses stretched out his hand over the sea; and the LORD swept the sea *back* by a strong east wind all night and turned the sea into dry land, so the waters were divided.

22 The sons of Israel went through the midst of the sea on the dry land, and the waters *were like* a wall to them on their right hand and on their left.

23 Then the Egyptians took up the pursuit, and all Pharaoh's horses, his chariots and his horsemen went in after them into the midst of the sea.

24 At the morning watch, the LORD looked down on the army of the Egyptians through the pillar of fire and cloud and brought the army of the Egyptians into confusion.

25 He caused their chariot wheels to swerve, and He made them drive with difficulty; so the Egyptians said, "Let us flee from Israel, for the LORD is fighting for them against the Egyptians."

26 Then the LORD said to Moses, "Stretch out your hand over the sea so that the waters may come back over the Egyptians, over their chariots and their horsemen."

27 So Moses stretched out his hand over the sea, and the sea returned to its normal state at daybreak, while the Egyptians were fleeing right into it; then the LORD overthrew the Egyptians in the midst of the sea.

28 The waters returned and covered the chariots and the horsemen, even Pharaoh's entire army that had gone into the sea after them; not even one of them remained.

29 But the sons of Israel walked on dry land through the midst of the sea, and the waters *were like* a wall to them on their right hand and on their left.

30 Thus the LORD saved Israel that day from the hand of the Egyptians, and Israel saw the Egyptians dead on the seashore.

31 When Israel saw the great power which the LORD had used against the Egyptians, the people feared the LORD, and they believed in the LORD and in His servant Moses.

282   © 2008 Precept Ministries International

EXODUS 15
Observation Worksheet

Chapter Theme _____

THEN Moses and the sons of Israel sang this song to the LORD, and said, "I will
     sing to the LORD, for He is highly exalted;
       The horse and its rider He has hurled into the sea.

2   "The LORD is my strength and song,

     And He has become my salvation;

     This is my God, and I will praise Him;

     My father's God, and I will extol Him.

3   "The LORD is a warrior;

     The LORD is His name.

4   "Pharaoh's chariots and his army He has cast into the sea;

     And the choicest of his officers are drowned in the Red Sea.

5   "The deeps cover them;

     They went down into the depths like a stone.

6   "Your right hand, O LORD, is majestic in power,

     Your right hand, O LORD, shatters the enemy.

7   "And in the greatness of Your excellence You overthrow those who rise up against You; You

     send forth Your burning anger, *and* it consumes them as chaff.

8   "At the blast of Your nostrils the waters were piled up,

     The flowing waters stood up like a heap;

     The deeps were congealed in the heart of the sea.

9   "The enemy said, 'I will pursue, I will overtake, I will divide the spoil;

     My desire shall be gratified against them;

     I will draw out my sword, my hand will destroy them.'

10   "You blew with Your wind, the sea covered them;

     They sank like lead in the mighty waters.

11   "Who is like You among the gods, O LORD?

© 2008 Precept Ministries International

Who is like You, majestic in holiness,

Awesome in praises, working wonders?

12 "You stretched out Your right hand,

The earth swallowed them.

13 "In Your lovingkindness You have led the people whom You have redeemed;

In Your strength You have guided *them* to Your holy habitation.

14 "The peoples have heard, they tremble;

Anguish has gripped the inhabitants of Philistia.

15 "Then the chiefs of Edom were dismayed;

The leaders of Moab, trembling grips them;

All the inhabitants of Canaan have melted away.

16 "Terror and dread fall upon them;

By the greatness of Your arm they are motionless as stone;

Until Your people pass over, O LORD,

Until the people pass over whom You have purchased.

17 "You will bring them and plant them in the mountain of Your inheritance,

The place, O LORD, which You have made for Your dwelling,

The sanctuary, O Lord, which Your hands have established.

18 "The LORD shall reign forever and ever."

19 For the horses of Pharaoh with his chariots and his horsemen went into the sea, and the LORD brought back the waters of the sea on them, but the sons of Israel walked on dry land through the midst of the sea.

20 Miriam the prophetess, Aaron's sister, took the timbrel in her hand, and all the women went out after her with timbrels and with dancing.

21 Miriam answered them,

"Sing to the LORD, for He is highly exalted;

The horse and his rider He has hurled into the sea."

22 Then Moses led Israel from the Red Sea, and they went out into the wilderness of Shur; and they went three days in the wilderness and found no water.

23 When they came to Marah, they could not drink the waters of Marah, for they

© *2008 Precept Ministries International*

were bitter ; therefore it was named Marah.

24   So the people grumbled at Moses, saying, "What shall we drink?"

25   Then he cried out to the LORD, and the LORD showed him a tree; and he threw *it* into the waters, and the waters became sweet. There He made for them a statute and regulation, and there He tested them.

26   And He said, "If you will give earnest heed to the voice of the LORD your God, and do what is right in His sight, and give ear to His commandments, and keep all His statutes, I will put none of the diseases on you which I have put on the Egyptians; for I, the LORD, am your healer."

27   Then they came to Elim where there *were* twelve springs of water and seventy date palms, and they camped there beside the waters.

© 2008 Precept Ministries International

© *2008 Precept Ministries International*

EXODUS 16
Observation Worksheet

Chapter Theme _____

THEN they set out from Elim, and all the congregation of the sons of Israel came to the wilderness of Sin, which is between Elim and Sinai, on the fifteenth day of the second month after their departure from the land of Egypt.

2   The whole congregation of the sons of Israel grumbled against Moses and Aaron in the wilderness.

3   The sons of Israel said to them, "Would that we had died by the LORD'S hand in the land of Egypt, when we sat by the pots of meat, when we ate bread to the full; for you have brought us out into this wilderness to kill this whole assembly with hunger."

4   Then the LORD said to Moses, "Behold, I will rain bread from heaven for you; and the people shall go out and gather a day's portion every day, that I may test them, whether or not they will walk in My instruction.

5   "On the sixth day, when they prepare what they bring in, it will be twice as much as they gather daily."

6   So Moses and Aaron said to all the sons of Israel, "At evening you will know that the LORD has brought you out of the land of Egypt;

7   and in the morning you will see the glory of the LORD, for He hears your grumblings against the LORD; and what are we, that you grumble against us?"

8   Moses said, "*This will happen* when the LORD gives you meat to eat in the evening, and bread to the full in the morning; for the LORD hears your grumblings which you grumble against Him. And what are we? Your grumblings are not against us but against the LORD."

9   Then Moses said to Aaron, "Say to all the congregation of the sons of Israel, 'Come near before the LORD, for He has heard your grumblings.'"

10   It came about as Aaron spoke to the whole congregation of the sons of Israel, that they looked toward the wilderness, and behold, the glory of the LORD appeared in the cloud.

11   And the LORD spoke to Moses, saying,

12   "I have heard the grumblings of the sons of Israel; speak to them, saying, 'At twilight you shall eat meat, and in the morning you shall be filled with bread; and you shall know that I am the LORD your God.'"

13   So it came about at evening that the quails came up and covered the camp, and in the morning there was a layer of dew around the camp.

14   When the layer of dew evaporated, behold, on the surface of the wilderness there was a fine flake-like thing, fine as the frost on the ground.

15   When the sons of Israel saw *it,* they said to one another, "What is it?" For they did not know what it was. And Moses said to them, "It is the bread which the LORD has given you to eat.

16   "This is what the LORD has commanded, 'Gather of it every man as much as he should eat; you shall take an omer apiece according to the number of persons each of you has in his tent.' "

17   The sons of Israel did so, and *some* gathered much and *some* little.

18   When they measured it with an omer, he who had gathered much had no excess, and he who had gathered little had no lack; every man gathered as much as he should eat.

19   Moses said to them, "Let no man leave any of it until morning."

20   But they did not listen to Moses, and some left part of it until morning, and it bred worms and became foul; and Moses was angry with them.

21   They gathered it morning by morning, every man as much as he should eat; but when the sun grew hot, it would melt.

22   Now on the sixth day they gathered twice as much bread, two omers for each one. When all the leaders of the congregation came and told Moses,

23   then he said to them, "This is what the LORD meant : Tomorrow is a sabbath observance, a holy sabbath to the LORD. Bake what you will bake and boil what you will boil, and all that is left over put aside to be kept until morning."

24   So they put it aside until morning, as Moses had ordered, and it did not become foul nor was there any worm in it.

                                        © *2008 Precept Ministries International*

25   Moses said, "Eat it today, for today is a sabbath to the LORD; today you will not find it in the field.

26   "Six days you shall gather it, but on the seventh day, *the* sabbath, there will be none."

27   It came about on the seventh day that some of the people went out to gather, but they found none.

28   Then the LORD said to Moses, "How long do you refuse to keep My commandments and My instructions ?

29   "See, the LORD has given you the sabbath; therefore He gives you bread for two days on the sixth day. Remain every man in his place; let no man go out of his place on the seventh day."

30   So the people rested on the seventh day.

31   The house of Israel named it manna, and it was like coriander seed, white, and its taste was like wafers with honey.

32   Then Moses said, "This is what the LORD has commanded, 'Let an omerful of it be kept throughout your generations, that they may see the bread that I fed you in the wilderness, when I brought you out of the land of Egypt.'"

33   Moses said to Aaron, "Take a jar and put an omerful of manna in it, and place it before the LORD to be kept throughout your generations."

34   As the LORD commanded Moses, so Aaron placed it before the Testimony, to be kept.

35   The sons of Israel ate the manna forty years, until they came to an inhabited land; they ate the manna until they came to the border of the land of Canaan.

36   (Now an omer is a tenth of an ephah.

© *2008 Precept Ministries International*

 © 2008 Precept Ministries International

EXODUS 17
Observation Worksheet

Chapter Theme _____

THEN all the congregation of the sons of Israel journeyed by stages from the wilderness of Sin, according to the command of the LORD, and camped at Rephidim, and there was no water for the people to drink.

2   Therefore the people quarreled with Moses and said, "Give us water that we may drink." And Moses said to them, "Why do you quarrel with me? Why do you test the LORD?"

3   But the people thirsted there for water; and they grumbled against Moses and said, "Why, now, have you brought us up from Egypt, to kill us and our children and our livestock with thirst?"

4   So Moses cried out to the LORD, saying, "What shall I do to this people? A little more and they will stone me."

5   Then the LORD said to Moses, "Pass before the people and take with you some of the elders of Israel; and take in your hand your staff with which you struck the Nile, and go.

6   "Behold, I will stand before you there on the rock at Horeb; and you shall strike the rock, and water will come out of it, that the people may drink." And Moses did so in the sight of the elders of Israel.

7   He named the place Massah and Meribah because of the quarrel of the sons of Israel, and because they tested the LORD, saying, "Is the LORD among us, or not?"

8   Then Amalek came and fought against Israel at Rephidim.

9   So Moses said to Joshua, "Choose men for us and go out, fight against Amalek. Tomorrow I will station myself on the top of the hill with the staff of God in my hand."

10   Joshua did as Moses told him, and fought against Amalek; and Moses, Aaron, and Hur went up to the top of the hill.

11   So it came about when Moses held his hand up, that Israel prevailed, and when he let his hand down, Amalek prevailed.

© 2008 Precept Ministries International

12   But Moses' hands were heavy. Then they took a stone and put it under him, and he sat on it; and Aaron and Hur supported his hands, one on one side and one on the other. Thus his hands were steady until the sun set.

13   So Joshua overwhelmed Amalek and his people with the edge of the sword.

14   Then the LORD said to Moses, "Write this in a book as a memorial and recite it to Joshua, that I will utterly blot out the memory of Amalek from under heaven."

15   Moses built an altar and named it The LORD is My Banner;

16   and he said, "The LORD has sworn; the LORD will have war against Amalek from generation to generation."

© *2008 Precept Ministries International*

EXODUS 18
Observation Worksheet

Chapter Theme _____

NOW Jethro, the priest of Midian, Moses' father-in-law, heard of all that God had done for Moses and for Israel His people, how the LORD had brought Israel out of Egypt.

2   Jethro, Moses' father-in-law, took Moses' wife Zipporah, after he had sent her away,

3   and her two sons, of whom one was named Gershom, for Moses said, "I have been a sojourner in a foreign land."

4   The other was named Eliezer, for *he said,* "The God of my father was my help, and delivered me from the sword of Pharaoh."

5   Then Jethro, Moses' father-in-law, came with his sons and his wife to Moses in the wilderness where he was camped, at the mount of God.

6   He sent word to Moses, "I, your father-in-law Jethro, am coming to you with your wife and her two sons with her."

7   Then Moses went out to meet his father-in-law, and he bowed down and kissed him; and they asked each other of their welfare and went into the tent.

8   Moses told his father-in-law all that the LORD had done to Pharaoh and to the Egyptians for Israel's sake, all the hardship that had befallen them on the journey, and *how* the LORD had delivered them.

9   Jethro rejoiced over all the goodness which the LORD had done to Israel, in delivering them from the hand of the Egyptians.

10   So Jethro said, "Blessed be the LORD who delivered you from the hand of the Egyptians and from the hand of Pharaoh, *and* who delivered the people from under the hand of the Egyptians.

11   "Now I know that the LORD is greater than all the gods; indeed, it was proven when they dealt proudly against the people."

12   Then Jethro, Moses' father-in-law, took a burnt offering and sacrifices for God, and Aaron came with all the elders of Israel to eat a meal with Moses' father-in-law before God.

13   It came about the next day that Moses sat to judge the people, and the people

stood about Moses from the morning until the evening.

14   Now when Moses' father-in-law saw all that he was doing for the people, he said, "What is this thing that you are doing for the people? Why do you alone sit *as judge* and all the people stand about you from morning until evening?"

15   Moses said to his father-in-law, "Because the people come to me to inquire of God.

16   "When they have a dispute, it comes to me, and I judge between a man and his neighbor and make known the statutes of God and His laws."

17   Moses' father-in-law said to him, "The thing that you are doing is not good.

18   "You will surely wear out, both yourself and these people who are with you, for the task is too heavy for you; you cannot do it alone.

19   "Now listen to me : I will give you counsel, and God be with you. You be the people's representative before God, and you bring the disputes to God,

20   then teach them the statutes and the laws, and make known to them the way in which they are to walk and the work they are to do.

21   "Furthermore, you shall select out of all the people able men who fear God, men of truth, those who hate dishonest gain; and you shall place *these* over them *as* leaders of thousands, of hundreds, of fifties and of tens.

22   "Let them judge the people at all times; and let it be that every major dispute they will bring to you, but every minor dispute they themselves will judge. So it will be easier for you, and they will bear *the burden* with you.

23   "If you do this thing and God *so* commands you, then you will be able to endure, and all these people also will go to their place in peace."

24   So Moses listened to his father-in-law and did all that he had said.

25   Moses chose able men out of all Israel and made them heads over the people, leaders of thousands, of hundreds, of fifties and of tens.

26   They judged the people at all times; the difficult dispute they would bring to Moses, but every minor dispute they themselves would judge.

27   Then Moses bade his father-in-law farewell, and he went his way into his own land.

   © 2008 Precept Ministries International

EXODUS 19
Observation Worksheet

Chapter Theme _____

IN the third month after the sons of Israel had gone out of the land of Egypt, on that very day they came into the wilderness of Sinai.

2   When they set out from Rephidim, they came to the wilderness of Sinai and camped in the wilderness; and there Israel camped in front of the mountain.

3   Moses went up to God, and the LORD called to him from the mountain, saying, "Thus you shall say to the house of Jacob and tell the sons of Israel:

4   'You yourselves have seen what I did to the Egyptians, and *how* I bore you on eagles' wings, and brought you to Myself.

5   'Now then, if you will indeed obey My voice and keep My covenant, then you shall be My own possession among all the peoples, for all the earth is Mine;

6   and you shall be to Me a kingdom of priests and a holy nation.' These are the words that you shall speak to the sons of Israel."

7   So Moses came and called the elders of the people, and set before them all these words which the LORD had commanded him.

8   All the people answered together and said, "All that the LORD has spoken we will do!" And Moses brought back the words of the people to the LORD.

9   The LORD said to Moses, "Behold, I will come to you in a thick cloud, so that the people may hear when I speak with you and may also believe in you forever." Then Moses told the words of the people to the LORD.

10   The LORD also said to Moses, "Go to the people and consecrate them today and tomorrow, and let them wash their garments;

11   and let them be ready for the third day, for on the third day the LORD will come down on Mount Sinai in the sight of all the people.

12   "You shall set bounds for the people all around, saying, 'Beware that you do not go up on the mountain or touch the border of it; whoever touches the mountain shall surely be put to death.

13   'No hand shall touch him, but he shall surely be stoned or shot through; whether

© 2008 Precept Ministries International

beast or man, he shall not live.' When the ram's horn sounds a long blast, they shall come up to the mountain."

14   So Moses went down from the mountain to the people and consecrated the people, and they washed their garments.

15   He said to the people, "Be ready for the third day; do not go near a woman."

16   So it came about on the third day, when it was morning, that there were thunder and lightning flashes and a thick cloud upon the mountain and a very loud trumpet sound, so that all the people who *were* in the camp trembled.

17   And Moses brought the people out of the camp to meet God, and they stood at the foot of the mountain.

18   Now Mount Sinai *was* all in smoke because the LORD descended upon it in fire; and its smoke ascended like the smoke of a furnace, and the whole mountain quaked violently.

19   When the sound of the trumpet grew louder and louder, Moses spoke and God answered him with thunder.

20   The LORD came down on Mount Sinai, to the top of the mountain; and the LORD called Moses to the top of the mountain, and Moses went up.

21   Then the LORD spoke to Moses, "Go down, warn the people, so that they do not break through to the LORD to gaze, and many of them perish.

22   "Also let the priests who come near to the LORD consecrate themselves, or else the LORD will break out against them."

23   Moses said to the LORD, "The people cannot come up to Mount Sinai, for You warned us, saying, 'Set bounds about the mountain and consecrate it.' "

24   Then the LORD said to him, "Go down and come up *again,* you and Aaron with you; but do not let the priests and the people break through to come up to the LORD, or He will break forth upon them."

25   So Moses went down to the people and told them.

© *2008 Precept Ministries International*

EXODUS 20
Observation Worksheet

Chapter Theme _____

THEN God spoke all these words, saying,

2   "I am the LORD your God, who brought you out of the land of Egypt, out of the house of slavery.

3   "You shall have no other gods before Me.

4   "You shall not make for yourself an idol, or any likeness of what is in heaven above or on the earth beneath or in the water under the earth.

5   "You shall not worship them or serve them; for I, the LORD your God, am a jealous God, visiting the iniquity of the fathers on the children, on the third and the fourth generations of those who hate Me,

6   but showing lovingkindness to thousands, to those who love Me and keep My commandments.

7   "You shall not take the name of the LORD your God in vain, for the LORD will not leave him unpunished who takes His name in vain.

8   "Remember the sabbath day, to keep it holy.

9   "Six days you shall labor and do all your work,

10   but the seventh day is a sabbath of the Lord your God; in it you shall not do any work, you or your son or your daughter, your male or your female servant or your cattle or your sojourner who stays with you.

11   "For in six days the LORD made the heavens and the earth, the sea and all that is in them, and rested on the seventh day; therefore the LORD blessed the sabbath day and made it holy.

12   "Honor your father and your mother, that your days may be prolonged in the land which the LORD your God gives you.

13   "You shall not murder.

14   "You shall not commit adultery.

15   "You shall not steal.

16   "You shall not bear false witness against your neighbor.

17   "You shall not covet your neighbor's house; you shall not covet your neighbor's

wife or his male servant or his female servant or his ox or his donkey or anything that belongs to your neighbor."

18 All the people perceived the thunder and the lightning flashes and the sound of the trumpet and the mountain smoking; and when the people saw *it,* they trembled and stood at a distance.

19 Then they said to Moses, "Speak to us yourself and we will listen; but let not God speak to us, or we will die."

20 Moses said to the people, "Do not be afraid; for God has come in order to test you, and in order that the fear of Him may remain with you, so that you may not sin."

21 So the people stood at a distance, while Moses approached the thick cloud where God *was.*

22 Then the Lord said to Moses, "Thus you shall say to the sons of Israel, 'You yourselves have seen that I have spoken to you from heaven.

23 'You shall not make *other gods* besides Me; gods of silver or gods of gold, you shall not make for yourselves.

24 'You shall make an altar of earth for Me, and you shall sacrifice on it your burnt offerings and your peace offerings, your sheep and your oxen; in every place where I cause My name to be remembered, I will come to you and bless you.

25 'If you make an altar of stone for Me, you shall not build it of cut stones, for if you wield your tool on it, you will profane it.

26 'And you shall not go up by steps to My altar, so that your nakedness will not be exposed on it.'

© 2008 Precept Ministries International

EXODUS 21
Observation Worksheet

Chapter Theme _____

"NOW these are the ordinances which you are to set before them:

2   "If you buy a Hebrew slave, he shall serve for six years; but on the seventh he shall go out as a free man without payment.

3   "If he comes alone, he shall go out alone ; if he is the husband of a wife, then his wife shall go out with him.

4   "If his master gives him a wife, and she bears him sons or daughters, the wife and her children shall belong to her master, and he shall go out alone.

5   "But if the slave plainly says, 'I love my master, my wife and my children; I will not go out as a free man,'

6   then his master shall bring him to God, then he shall bring him to the door or the doorpost. And his master shall pierce his ear with an awl; and he shall serve him permanently.

7   "If a man sells his daughter as a female slave, she is not to go free as the male slaves do.

8   "If she is displeasing in the eyes of her master who designated her for himself, then he shall let her be redeemed. He does not have authority to sell her to a foreign people because of his unfairness to her.

9   "If he designates her for his son, he shall deal with her according to the custom of daughters.

10   "If he takes to himself another woman, he may not reduce her food, her clothing, or her conjugal rights.

11   "If he will not do these three *things* for her, then she shall go out for nothing, without *payment of* money.

12   "He who strikes a man so that he dies shall surely be put to death.

13   "But if he did not lie in wait *for him,* but God let *him* fall into his hand, then I will appoint you a place to which he may flee.

14   "If, however, a man acts presumptuously toward his neighbor, so as to kill him craftily, you are to take him *even* from My altar, that he may die.

15   "He who strikes his father or his mother shall surely be put to death.

Exodus
Exodus 21

16   "He who kidnaps a man, whether he sells him or he is found in his possession, shall
     surely be put to death.

17   "He who curses his father or his mother shall surely be put to death.

18   "If men have a quarrel and one strikes the other with a stone or with *his* fist, and he
     does not die but remains in bed,

19   if he gets up and walks around outside on his staff, then he who struck him shall
     go unpunished; he shall only pay for his loss of time, and shall take care of him
     until he is completely healed.

20   "If a man strikes his male or female slave with a rod and he dies at his hand, he
     shall be punished.

21   "If, however, he survives a day or two, no vengeance shall be taken; for he is his
     property.

22   "If men struggle with each other and strike a woman with child so that she gives
     birth prematurely, yet there is no injury, he shall surely be fined as the woman's
     husband may demand of him, and he shall pay as the judges *decide.*

23   "But if there is *any further* injury, then you shall appoint *as a penalty* life for life,

24   eye for eye, tooth for tooth, hand for hand, foot for foot,

25   burn for burn, wound for wound, bruise for bruise.

26   "If a man strikes the eye of his male or female slave, and destroys it, he shall let
     him go free on account of his eye.

27   "And if he knocks out a tooth of his male or female slave, he shall let him go free
     on account of his tooth.

28   "If an ox gores a man or a woman to death, the ox shall surely be stoned and its
     flesh shall not be eaten; but the owner of the ox shall go unpunished.

29   "If, however, an ox was previously in the habit of goring and its owner has been
     warned, yet he does not confine it and it kills a man or a woman, the ox shall be
     stoned and its owner also shall be put to death.

30   "If a ransom is demanded of him, then he shall give for the redemption of his life
     whatever is demanded of him.

31   "Whether it gores a son or a daughter, it shall be done to him according to the
     same rule.

32   "If the ox gores a male or female slave, the owner shall give his *or her* master
     thirty shekels of silver, and the ox shall be stoned.

33   "If a man opens a pit, or digs a pit and does not cover it over, and an ox or a don-
     key falls into it,

34   the owner of the pit shall make restitution; he shall give money to its owner, and
     the dead *animal* shall become his.

© *2008 Precept Ministries International*

35 "If one man's ox hurts another's so that it dies, then they shall sell the live ox and divide its price equally; and also they shall divide the dead *ox.*

36 "Or *if* it is known that the ox was previously in the habit of goring, yet its owner has not confined it, he shall surely pay ox for ox, and the dead *animal* shall become his.

© 2008 Precept Ministries International

 © 2008 Precept Ministries International

EXODUS 22
Observation Worksheet

Chapter Theme _____

IF a man steals an ox or a sheep and slaughters it or sells it, he shall pay five oxen for the ox and four sheep for the sheep.

2 "If the thief is caught while breaking in and is struck so that he dies, there will be no bloodguiltiness on his account.

3 "But if the sun has risen on him, there will be bloodguiltiness on his account. He shall surely make restitution; if he owns nothing, then he shall be sold for his theft.

4 "If what he stole is actually found alive in his possession, whether an ox or a donkey or a sheep, he shall pay double.

5 "If a man lets a field or vineyard be grazed *bare* and lets his animal loose so that it grazes in another man's field, he shall make restitution from the best of his own field and the best of his own vineyard.

6 "If a fire breaks out and spreads to thorn bushes, so that stacked grain or the standing grain or the field *itself* is consumed, he who started the fire shall surely make restitution.

7 "If a man gives his neighbor money or goods to keep *for him* and it is stolen from the man's house, if the thief is caught, he shall pay double.

8 "If the thief is not caught, then the owner of the house shall appear before the judges, *to* determine whether he laid his hands on his neighbor's property.

9 "For every breach of trust, *whether it is* for ox, for donkey, for sheep, for clothing, *or* for any lost thing about which one says, 'This is it,' the case of both parties shall come before the judges; he whom the judges condemn shall pay double to his neighbor.

10 "If a man gives his neighbor a donkey, an ox, a sheep, or any animal to keep *for him,* and it dies or is hurt or is driven away while no one is looking,

11 an oath before the LORD shall be made by the two of them that he has not laid

hands on his neighbor's property; and its owner shall accept *it,* and he shall not make restitution.

12 "But if it is actually stolen from him, he shall make restitution to its owner.

13 "If it is all torn to pieces, let him bring it as evidence; he shall not make restitution for what has been torn to pieces.

14 "If a man borrows *anything* from his neighbor, and it is injured or dies while its owner is not with it, he shall make full restitution.

15 "If its owner is with it, he shall not make restitution; if it is hired, it came for its hire.

16 "If a man seduces a virgin who is not engaged, and lies with her, he must pay a dowry for her *to be* his wife.

17 "If her father absolutely refuses to give her to him, he shall pay money equal to the dowry for virgins.

18 "You shall not allow a sorceress to live.

19 "Whoever lies with an animal shall surely be put to death.

20 "He who sacrifices to any god, other than to the Lord alone, shall be utterly destroyed.

21 "You shall not wrong a stranger or oppress him, for you were strangers in the land of Egypt.

22 "You shall not afflict any widow or orphan.

23 "If you afflict him at all, *and* if he does cry out to Me, I will surely hear his cry;

24 and My anger will be kindled, and I will kill you with the sword, and your wives shall become widows and your children fatherless.

25 "If you lend money to My people, to the poor among you, you are not to act as a creditor to him; you shall not charge him interest.

26 "If you ever take your neighbor's cloak as a pledge, you are to return it to him before the sun sets,

27 for that is his only covering; it is his cloak for his body. What else shall he sleep in? And it shall come about that when he cries out to Me, I will hear *him,* for I am gracious.

© *2008 Precept Ministries International*

28 "You shall not curse God, nor curse a ruler of your people.

29 "You shall not delay *the offering from* your harvest and your vintage. The first-born of your sons you shall give to Me.

30 "You shall do the same with your oxen *and* with your sheep. It shall be with its mother seven days; on the eighth day you shall give it to Me.

31 "You shall be holy men to Me, therefore you shall not eat *any* flesh torn to pieces in the field; you shall throw it to the dogs.

© *2008 Precept Ministries International*

© *2008 Precept Ministries International*

EXODUS 23
Observation Worksheet

Chapter Theme _____

"YOU shall not bear a false report; do not join your hand with a wicked man to be a malicious witness.

2   "You shall not follow the masses in doing evil, nor shall you testify in a dispute so as to turn aside after a multitude in order to pervert *justice;*

3   nor shall you be partial to a poor man in his dispute.

4   "If you meet your enemy's ox or his donkey wandering away, you shall surely return it to him.

5   "If you see the donkey of one who hates you lying *helpless* under its load, you shall refrain from leaving it to him, you shall surely release *it* with him.

6   "You shall not pervert the justice *due* to your needy *brother* in his dispute.

7   "Keep far from a false charge, and do not kill the innocent or the righteous, for I will not acquit the guilty.

8   "You shall not take a bribe, for a bribe blinds the clear-sighted and subverts the cause of the just.

9   "You shall not oppress a stranger, since you yourselves know the feelings of a stranger, for you *also* were strangers in the land of Egypt.

10   "You shall sow your land for six years and gather in its yield,

11   but *on* the seventh year you shall let it rest and lie fallow, so that the needy of your people may eat; and whatever they leave the beast of the field may eat. You are to do the same with your vineyard *and* your olive grove.

12   "Six days you are to do your work, but on the seventh day you shall cease *from labor* so that your ox and your donkey may rest, and the son of your female slave, as well as your stranger, may refresh themselves.

13   "Now concerning everything which I have said to you, be on your guard; and do not mention the name of other gods, nor let *them* be heard from your mouth.

14   "Three times a year you shall celebrate a feast to Me.

© 2008 Precept Ministries International

15 "You shall observe the Feast of Unleavened Bread; for seven days you are to eat unleavened bread, as I commanded you, at the appointed time in the month Abib, for in it you came out of Egypt. And none shall appear before Me empty-handed.

16 "Also *you shall observe* the Feast of the Harvest *of* the first fruits of your labors *from* what you sow in the field; also the Feast of the Ingathering at the end of the year when you gather in *the fruit of* your labors from the field.

17 "Three times a year all your males shall appear before the Lord GOD.

18 "You shall not offer the blood of My sacrifice with leavened bread; nor is the fat of My feast to remain overnight until morning.

19 "You shall bring the choice first fruits of your soil into the house of the LORD your God.
"You are not to boil a young goat in the milk of its mother.

20 "Behold, I am going to send an angel before you to guard you along the way and to bring you into the place which I have prepared.

21 "Be on your guard before him and obey his voice; do not be rebellious toward him, for he will not pardon your transgression, since My name is in him.

22 "But if you truly obey his voice and do all that I say, then I will be an enemy to your enemies and an adversary to your adversaries.

23 "For My angel will go before you and bring you in to *the land of* the Amorites, the Hittites, the Perizzites, the Canaanites, the Hivites and the Jebusites; and I will completely destroy them.

24 "You shall not worship their gods, nor serve them, nor do according to their deeds; but you shall utterly overthrow them and break their *sacred* pillars in pieces.

25 "But you shall serve the LORD your God, and He will bless your bread and your water; and I will remove sickness from your midst.

26 "There shall be no one miscarrying or barren in your land; I will fulfill the number of your days.

27 "I will send My terror ahead of you, and throw into confusion all the people among whom you come, and I will make all your enemies turn *their* backs to

© *2008 Precept Ministries International*

you.

28 "I will send hornets ahead of you so that they will drive out the Hivites, the Canaanites, and the Hittites before you.

29 "I will not drive them out before you in a single year, that the land may not become desolate and the beasts of the field become too numerous for you.

30 "I will drive them out before you little by little, until you become fruitful and take possession of the land.

31 "I will fix your boundary from the Red Sea to the sea of the Philistines, and from the wilderness to the River *Euphrates;* for I will deliver the inhabitants of the land into your hand, and you will drive them out before you.

32 "You shall make no covenant with them or with their gods.

33 "They shall not live in your land, because they will make you sin against Me; for *if* you serve their gods, it will surely be a snare to you."

© *2008 Precept Ministries International*

© *2008 Precept Ministries International*

EXODUS 24
Observation Worksheet

Chapter Theme _____

THEN He said to Moses, "Come up to the LORD, you and Aaron, Nadab and Abihu and seventy of the elders of Israel, and you shall worship at a distance.

2 "Moses alone, however, shall come near to the LORD, but they shall not come near, nor shall the people come up with him."

3 Then Moses came and recounted to the people all the words of the LORD and all the ordinances ; and all the people answered with one voice and said, "All the words which the LORD has spoken we will do!"

4 Moses wrote down all the words of the LORD. Then he arose early in the morning, and built an altar at the foot of the mountain with twelve pillars for the twelve tribes of Israel.

5 He sent young men of the sons of Israel, and they offered burnt offerings and sacrificed young bulls as peace offerings to the LORD.

6 Moses took half of the blood and put *it* in basins, and the *other* half of the blood he sprinkled on the altar.

7 Then he took the book of the covenant and read *it* in the hearing of the people; and they said, "All that the LORD has spoken we will do, and we will be obedient!"

8 So Moses took the blood and sprinkled *it* on the people, and said, "Behold the blood of the covenant, which the LORD has made with you in accordance with all these words."

9 Then Moses went up with Aaron, Nadab and Abihu, and seventy of the elders of Israel,

10 and they saw the God of Israel; and under His feet there appeared to be a pavement of sapphire, as clear as the sky itself.

11 Yet He did not stretch out His hand against the nobles of the sons of Israel; and they saw God, and they ate and drank.

12 Now the LORD said to Moses, "Come up to Me on the mountain and remain there, and I will give you the stone tablets with the law and the commandment which I have written for their instruction."

13   So Moses arose with Joshua his servant, and Moses went up to the mountain of God.

14   But to the elders he said, "Wait here for us until we return to you. And behold, Aaron and Hur are with you; whoever has a legal matter, let him approach them."

15   Then Moses went up to the mountain, and the cloud covered the mountain.

16   The glory of the LORD rested on Mount Sinai, and the cloud covered it for six days; and on the seventh day He called to Moses from the midst of the cloud.

17   And to the eyes of the sons of Israel the appearance of the glory of the LORD was like a consuming fire on the mountain top.

18   Moses entered the midst of the cloud as he went up to the mountain; and Moses was on the mountain forty days and forty nights.

                    © *2008 Precept Ministries International*

EXODUS 25
Observation Worksheet

Chapter Theme _____

THEN the LORD spoke to Moses, saying,

2   "Tell the sons of Israel to raise a contribution for Me; from every man whose heart moves him you shall raise My contribution.

3   "This is the contribution which you are to raise from them: gold, silver and bronze,

4   blue, purple and scarlet *material,* fine linen, goat *hair,*

5   rams' skins dyed red, porpoise skins, acacia wood,

6   oil for lighting, spices for the anointing oil and for the fragrant incense,

7   onyx stones and setting stones for the ephod and for the breastpiece.

8   "Let them construct a sanctuary for Me, that I may dwell among them.

9   "According to all that I am going to show you, *as* the pattern of the tabernacle and the pattern of all its furniture, just so you shall construct *it.*

10   "They shall construct an ark of acacia wood two and a half cubits long, and one and a half cubits wide, and one and a half cubits high.

11   "You shall overlay it with pure gold, inside and out you shall overlay it, and you shall make a gold molding around it.

12   "You shall cast four gold rings for it and fasten them on its four feet, and two rings shall be on one side of it and two rings on the other side of it.

13   "You shall make poles of acacia wood and overlay them with gold.

14   "You shall put the poles into the rings on the sides of the ark, to carry the ark with them.

15   "The poles shall remain in the rings of the ark; they shall not be removed from it.

16   "You shall put into the ark the testimony which I shall give you.

17   "You shall make a mercy seat of pure gold, two and a half cubits long and one and a half cubits wide.

18   "You shall make two cherubim of gold, make them of hammered work at the two ends of the mercy seat.

19   "Make one cherub at one end and one cherub at the other end; you shall make the cherubim *of one piece* with the mercy seat at its two ends.

20   "The cherubim shall have *their* wings spread upward, covering the mercy seat with their wings and facing one another; the faces of the cherubim are to be *turned* toward the mercy seat.

21   "You shall put the mercy seat on top of the ark, and in the ark you shall put the testimony which I will give to you.

22   "There I will meet with you; and from above the mercy seat, from between the two cherubim which are upon the ark of the testimony, I will speak to you about all that I will give you in commandment for the sons of Israel.

23   "You shall make a table of acacia wood, two cubits long and one cubit wide and one and a half cubits high.

24   "You shall overlay it with pure gold and make a gold border around it.

25   "You shall make for it a rim of a handbreadth around *it;* and you shall make a gold border for the rim around it.

26   "You shall make four gold rings for it and put rings on the four corners which are on its four feet.

27   "The rings shall be close to the rim as holders for the poles to carry the table.

28   "You shall make the poles of acacia wood and overlay them with gold, so that with them the table may be carried.

29   "You shall make its dishes and its pans and its jars and its bowls with which to pour drink offerings; you shall make them of pure gold.

30   "You shall set the bread of the Presence on the table before Me at all times.

31   "Then you shall make a lampstand of pure gold. The lampstand *and* its base and its shaft are to be made of hammered work; its cups, its bulbs and its flowers shall be *of one piece* with it.

32   "Six branches shall go out from its sides; three branches of the lampstand from its one

© *2008 Precept Ministries International*

side and three branches of the lampstand from its other side.

33   "Three cups *shall be* shaped like almond *blossoms* in the one branch, a bulb and a flower, and three cups shaped like almond *blossoms* in the other branch, a bulb and a flower—so for six branches going out from the lampstand;

34   and in the lampstand four cups shaped like almond *blossoms,* its bulbs and its flowers.

35   "A bulb shall be under the *first* pair of branches *coming* out of it, and a bulb under the *second* pair of branches *coming* out of it, and a bulb under the *third* pair of branches *coming* out of it, for the six branches coming out of the lampstand.

36   "Their bulbs and their branches *shall be of one piece* with it; all of it shall be one piece of hammered work of pure gold.

37   "Then you shall make its lamps seven *in number;* and they shall mount its lamps so as to shed light on the space in front of it.

38   "Its snuffers and their trays *shall be* of pure gold.

39   "It shall be made from a talent of pure gold, with all these utensils.

40   "See that you make *them* after the pattern for them, which was shown to you on the mountain.

© 2008 Precept Ministries International

© 2008 Precept Ministries International

EXODUS 26
Observation Worksheet

Chapter Theme _____

"MOREOVER you shall make the tabernacle with ten curtains of fine twisted linen and blue and purple and scarlet *material;* you shall make them with cherubim, the work of a skillful workman.

2   "The length of each curtain shall be twenty-eight cubits, and the width of each curtain four cubits ; all the curtains shall have the same measurements.

3   "Five curtains shall be joined to one another, and *the other* five curtains *shall be* joined to one another.

4   "You shall make loops of blue on the edge of the outermost curtain in the *first* set, and likewise you shall make *them* on the edge of the curtain that is outermost in the second set.

5   "You shall make fifty loops in the one curtain, and you shall make fifty loops on the edge of the curtain that is in the second set ; the loops shall be opposite each other.

6   "You shall make fifty clasps of gold, and join the curtains to one another with the clasps so that the tabernacle will be a unit.

7   "Then you shall make curtains of goats' *hair* for a tent over the tabernacle; you shall make eleven curtains in all.

8   "The length of each curtain *shall be* thirty cubits, and the width of each curtain four cubits; the eleven curtains shall have the same measurements.

9   "You shall join five curtains by themselves and the *other* six curtains by themselves, and you shall double over the sixth curtain at the front of the tent.

10   "You shall make fifty loops on the edge of the curtain that is outermost in the *first* set, and fifty loops on the edge of the curtain *that is outermost in* the second set.

11   "You shall make fifty clasps of bronze, and you shall put the clasps into the loops and join the tent together so that it will be a unit.

12   "The overlapping part that is left over in the curtains of the tent, the half curtain that is left over, shall lap over the back of the tabernacle.

13   "The cubit on one side and the cubit on the other, of what is left over in the length of the curtains of the tent, shall lap over the sides of the tabernacle on one side and on the other, to cover it.

14   "You shall make a covering for the tent of rams' skins dyed red and a covering of porpoise skins above.

15   "Then you shall make the boards for the tabernacle of acacia wood, standing upright.

16   "Ten cubits *shall be* the length of each board and one and a half cubits the width of each board.

17   "*There shall be* two tenons for each board, fitted to one another; thus you shall do for all the boards of the tabernacle.

18   "You shall make the boards for the tabernacle: twenty boards for the south side.

19   "You shall make forty sockets of silver under the twenty boards, two sockets under one board for its two tenons and two sockets under another board for its two tenons;

20   and for the second side of the tabernacle, on the north side, twenty boards,

21   and their forty sockets of silver; two sockets under one board and two sockets under another board.

22   "For the rear of the tabernacle, to the west, you shall make six boards.

23   "You shall make two boards for the corners of the tabernacle at the rear.

24   "They shall be double beneath, and together they shall be complete to its top to the first ring; thus it shall be with both of them: they shall form the two corners.

25   "There shall be eight boards with their sockets of silver, sixteen sockets ; two sockets under one board and two sockets under another board.

26   "Then you shall make bars of acacia wood, five for the boards of one side of the tabernacle,

27   and five bars for the boards of the other side of the tabernacle, and five bars for the

© *2008 Precept Ministries International*

boards of the side of the tabernacle for the rear *side* to the west.

28 "The middle bar in the center of the boards shall pass through from end to end.

29 "You shall overlay the boards with gold and make their rings of gold *as* holders for the bars; and you shall overlay the bars with gold.

30 "Then you shall erect the tabernacle according to its plan which you have been shown in the mountain.

31 "You shall make a veil of blue and purple and scarlet *material* and fine twisted linen; it shall be made with cherubim, the work of a skillful workman.

32 "You shall hang it on four pillars of acacia overlaid with gold, their hooks *also being of* gold, on four sockets of silver.

33 "You shall hang up the veil under the clasps, and shall bring in the ark of the testimony there within the veil; and the veil shall serve for you as a partition between the holy place and the holy of holies.

34 "You shall put the mercy seat on the ark of the testimony in the holy of holies.

35 "You shall set the table outside the veil, and the lampstand opposite the table on the side of the tabernacle toward the south; and you shall put the table on the north side.

36 "You shall make a screen for the doorway of the tent of blue and purple and scarlet *material* and fine twisted linen, the work of a weaver.

37 "You shall make five pillars of acacia for the screen and overlay them with gold, their hooks *also being of* gold; and you shall cast five sockets of bronze for them.

© 2008 Precept Ministries International

© 2008 Precept Ministries International

EXODUS 27
Observation Worksheet

Chapter Theme _____

"AND you shall make the altar of acacia wood, five cubits long and five cubits wide; the altar shall be square, and its height shall be three cubits.

2 "You shall make its horns on its four corners; its horns shall be of one piece with it, and you shall overlay it with bronze.

3 "You shall make its pails for removing its ashes, and its shovels and its basins and its forks and its firepans; you shall make all its utensils of bronze.

4 "You shall make for it a grating of network of bronze, and on the net you shall make four bronze rings at its four corners.

5 "You shall put it beneath, under the ledge of the altar, so that the net will reach halfway up the altar.

6 "You shall make poles for the altar, poles of acacia wood, and overlay them with bronze.

7 "Its poles shall be inserted into the rings, so that the poles shall be on the two sides of the altar when it is carried.

8 "You shall make it hollow with planks; as it was shown to you in the mountain, so they shall make *it*.

9 "You shall make the court of the tabernacle. On the south side *there shall be* hangings for the court of fine twisted linen one hundred cubits long for one side;

10 and its pillars *shall be* twenty, with their twenty sockets of bronze; the hooks of the pillars and their bands *shall be* of silver.

11 "Likewise for the north side in length *there shall be* hangings one hundred *cubits* long, and its twenty pillars with their twenty sockets of bronze; the hooks of the pillars and their bands *shall be* of silver.

12 "*For* the width of the court on the west side *shall be* hangings of fifty cubits *with* their ten pillars and their ten sockets.

13 "The width of the court on the east side *shall be* fifty cubits.

14 "The hangings for the *one* side *of the gate shall be* fifteen cubits *with* their three pillars and their three sockets.

© 2008 Precept Ministries International

15 "And for the other side *shall be* hangings of fifteen cubits *with* their three pillars and their three sockets.

16 "For the gate of the court *there shall be* a screen of twenty cubits, of blue and purple and scarlet *material* and fine twisted linen, the work of a weaver, *with* their four pillars and their four sockets.

17 "All the pillars around the court shall be furnished with silver bands *with* their hooks of silver and their sockets of bronze.

18 "The length of the court *shall be* one hundred cubits, and the width fifty throughout, and the height five cubits of fine twisted linen, and their sockets of bronze.

19 "All the utensils of the tabernacle *used* in all its service, and all its pegs, and all the pegs of the court, *shall be* of bronze.

20 "You shall charge the sons of Israel, that they bring you clear oil of beaten olives for the light, to make a lamp burn continually.

21 "In the tent of meeting, outside the veil which is before the testimony, Aaron and his sons shall keep it in order from evening to morning before the LORD; *it shall be* a perpetual statute throughout their generations for the sons of Israel.

© *2008 Precept Ministries International*

EXODUS 28
Observation Worksheet

Chapter Theme _____

"THEN bring near to yourself Aaron your brother, and his sons with him, from among the sons of Israel, to minister as priest to Me—Aaron, Nadab and Abihu, Eleazar and Ithamar, Aaron's sons.

2   "You shall make holy garments for Aaron your brother, for glory and for beauty.

3   "You shall speak to all the skillful persons whom I have endowed with the spirit of wisdom, that they make Aaron's garments to consecrate him, that he may minister as priest to Me.

4   "These are the garments which they shall make: a breastpiece and an ephod and a robe and a tunic of checkered work, a turban and a sash, and they shall make holy garments for Aaron your brother and his sons, that he may minister as priest to Me.

5   "They shall take the gold and the blue and the purple and the scarlet *material* and the fine linen.

6   "They shall also make the ephod of gold, of blue and purple *and* scarlet *material* and fine twisted linen, the work of the skillful workman.

7   "It shall have two shoulder pieces joined to its two ends, that it may be joined.

8   "The skillfully woven band, which is on it, shall be like its workmanship, of the same material: of gold, of blue and purple and scarlet *material* and fine twisted linen.

9   "You shall take two onyx stones and engrave on them the names of the sons of Israel,

10   six of their names on the one stone and the names of the remaining six on the other stone, according to their birth.

11   "As a jeweler engraves a signet, you shall engrave the two stones according to the names of the sons of Israel; you shall set them in filigree *settings* of gold.

12   "You shall put the two stones on the shoulder pieces of the ephod, *as* stones of memorial for the sons of Israel, and Aaron shall bear their names before the Lord on his two shoulders for a memorial.

13   "You shall make filigree *settings* of gold,

14   and two chains of pure gold; you shall make them of twisted cordage work, and you shall put the corded chains on the filigree *settings.*

15   "You shall make a breastpiece of judgment, the work of a skillful workman; like the work of the ephod you shall make it: of gold, of blue and purple and scarlet *material* and fine twisted linen you shall make it.

16   "It shall be square *and* folded double, a span in length and a span in width.

17   "You shall mount on it four rows of stones; the first row *shall be* a row of ruby, topaz and emerald;

18   and the second row a turquoise, a sapphire and a diamond;

19   and the third row a jacinth, an agate and an amethyst;

20   and the fourth row a beryl and an onyx and a jasper; they shall be set in gold filigree.

21   "The stones shall be according to the names of the sons of Israel: twelve, according to their names; they shall be *like* the engravings of a seal, each according to his name for the twelve tribes.

22   "You shall make on the breastpiece chains of twisted cordage work in pure gold.

23   "You shall make on the breastpiece two rings of gold, and shall put the two rings on the two ends of the breastpiece.

24   "You shall put the two cords of gold on the two rings at the ends of the breastpiece.

25   "You shall put the *other* two ends of the two cords on the two filigree *settings,* and put them on the shoulder pieces of the ephod, at the front of it.

26   "You shall make two rings of gold and shall place them on the two ends of the breastpiece, on the edge of it, which is toward the inner side of the ephod.

27   "You shall make two rings of gold and put them on the bottom of the two shoulder pieces of the ephod, on the front of it close to the place where it is joined, above the skillfully woven band of the ephod.

28   "They shall bind the breastpiece by its rings to the rings of the ephod with a blue cord, so that it will be on the skillfully woven band of the ephod, and that the

© *2008 Precept Ministries International*

breastpiece will not come loose from the ephod.

29 "Aaron shall carry the names of the sons of Israel in the breastpiece of judgment over his heart when he enters the holy place, for a memorial before the LORD continually.

30 "You shall put in the breastpiece of judgment the Urim and the Thummim, and they shall be over Aaron's heart when he goes in before the LORD; and Aaron shall carry the judgment of the sons of Israel over his heart before the LORD continually.

31 "You shall make the robe of the ephod all of blue.

32 "There shall be an opening at its top in the middle of it; around its opening there shall be a binding of woven work, like the opening of a coat of mail, so that it will not be torn.

33 "You shall make on its hem pomegranates of blue and purple and scarlet *material,* all around on its hem, and bells of gold between them all around:

34 a golden bell and a pomegranate, a golden bell and a pomegranate, all around on the hem of the robe.

35 "It shall be on Aaron when he ministers; and its tinkling shall be heard when he enters and leaves the holy place before the LORD, so that he will not die.

36 "You shall also make a plate of pure gold and shall engrave on it, like the engravings of a seal, 'Holy to the LORD.'

37 "You shall fasten it on a blue cord, and it shall be on the turban; it shall be at the front of the turban.

38 "It shall be on Aaron's forehead, and Aaron shall take away the iniquity of the holy things which the sons of Israel consecrate, with regard to all their holy gifts; and it shall always be on his forehead, that they may be accepted before the LORD.

39 "You shall weave the tunic of checkered work of fine linen, and shall make a turban of fine linen, and you shall make a sash, the work of a weaver.

40 "For Aaron's sons you shall make tunics; you shall also make sashes for them, and you shall make caps for them, for glory and for beauty.

© *2008 Precept Ministries International*

41 "You shall put them on Aaron your brother and on his sons with him; and you shall anoint them and ordain them and consecrate them, that they may serve Me as priests.

42 "You shall make for them linen breeches to cover *their* bare flesh; they shall reach from the loins even to the thighs.

43 "They shall be on Aaron and on his sons when they enter the tent of meeting, or when they approach the altar to minister in the holy place, so that they do not incur guilt and die. It *shall be* a statute forever to him and to his descendants after him.

© *2008 Precept Ministries International*

EXODUS 29
Observation Worksheet

Chapter Theme _____

"NOW this is what you shall do to them to consecrate them to minister as priests to Me: take one young bull and two rams without blemish,

2 and unleavened bread and unleavened cakes mixed with oil, and unleavened wafers spread with oil; you shall make them of fine wheat flour.

3 "You shall put them in one basket, and present them in the basket along with the bull and the two rams.

4 "Then you shall bring Aaron and his sons to the doorway of the tent of meeting and wash them with water.

5 "You shall take the garments, and put on Aaron the tunic and the robe of the ephod and the ephod and the breastpiece, and gird him with the skillfully woven band of the ephod;

6 and you shall set the turban on his head and put the holy crown on the turban.

7 "Then you shall take the anointing oil and pour it on his head and anoint him.

8 "You shall bring his sons and put tunics on them.

9 "You shall gird them with sashes, Aaron and his sons, and bind caps on them, and they shall have the priesthood by a perpetual statute. So you shall ordain Aaron and his sons.

10 "Then you shall bring the bull before the tent of meeting, and Aaron and his sons shall lay their hands on the head of the bull.

11 "You shall slaughter the bull before the LORD at the doorway of the tent of meeting.

12 "You shall take some of the blood of the bull and put *it* on the horns of the altar with your finger; and you shall pour out all the blood at the base of the altar.

13 "You shall take all the fat that covers the entrails and the lobe of the liver, and the two kidneys and the fat that is on them, and offer them up in smoke on the altar.

14 "But the flesh of the bull and its hide and its refuse, you shall burn with fire out-

© 2008 Precept Ministries International

side the camp; it is a sin offering.

15   "You shall also take the one ram, and Aaron and his sons shall lay their hands on the head of the ram;

16   and you shall slaughter the ram and shall take its blood and sprinkle it around on the altar.

17   "Then you shall cut the ram into its pieces, and wash its entrails and its legs, and put *them* with its pieces and its head.

18   "You shall offer up in smoke the whole ram on the altar; it is a burnt offering to the LORD: it is a soothing aroma, an offering by fire to the LORD.

19   "Then you shall take the other ram, and Aaron and his sons shall lay their hands on the head of the ram.

20   "You shall slaughter the ram, and take some of its blood and put *it* on the lobe of Aaron's right ear and on the lobes of his sons' right ears and on the thumbs of their right hands and on the big toes of their right feet, and sprinkle the *rest of the* blood around on the altar.

21   "Then you shall take some of the blood that is on the altar and some of the anointing oil, and sprinkle *it* on Aaron and on his garments and on his sons and on his sons' garments with him; so he and his garments shall be consecrated, as well as his sons and his sons' garments with him.

22   "You shall also take the fat from the ram and the fat tail, and the fat that covers the entrails and the lobe of the liver, and the two kidneys and the fat that is on them and the right thigh (for it is a ram of ordination),

23   and one cake of bread and one cake of bread *mixed with* oil and one wafer from the basket of unleavened bread which is *set* before the LORD;

24   and you shall put all these in the hands of Aaron and in the hands of his sons, and shall wave them as a wave offering before the LORD.

25   "You shall take them from their hands, and offer them up in smoke on the altar on the burnt offering for a soothing aroma before the LORD; it is an offering by fire to the LORD.

26   "Then you shall take the breast of Aaron's ram of ordination, and wave it as a

© *2008 Precept Ministries International*

wave offering before the LORD; and it shall be your portion.

27 "You shall consecrate the breast of the wave offering and the thigh of the heave offering which was waved and which was offered from the ram of ordination, from the one which was for Aaron and from the one which was for his sons.

28 "It shall be for Aaron and his sons as *their* portion forever from the sons of Israel, for it is a heave offering; and it shall be a heave offering from the sons of Israel from the sacrifices of their peace offerings, *even* their heave offering to the LORD.

29 "The holy garments of Aaron shall be for his sons after him, that in them they may be anointed and ordained.

30 "For seven days the one of his sons who is priest in his stead shall put them on when he enters the tent of meeting to minister in the holy place.

31 "You shall take the ram of ordination and boil its flesh in a holy place.

32 "Aaron and his sons shall eat the flesh of the ram and the bread that is in the basket, at the doorway of the tent of meeting.

33 "Thus they shall eat those things by which atonement was made at their ordination *and* consecration; but a layman shall not eat *them,* because they are holy.

34 "If any of the flesh of ordination or any of the bread remains until morning, then you shall burn the remainder with fire; it shall not be eaten, because it is holy.

35 "Thus you shall do to Aaron and to his sons, according to all that I have commanded you; you shall ordain them through seven days.

36 "Each day you shall offer a bull as a sin offering for atonement, and you shall purify the altar when you make atonement for it, and you shall anoint it to consecrate it.

37 "For seven days you shall make atonement for the altar and consecrate it; then the altar shall be most holy, *and* whatever touches the altar shall be holy.

38 "Now this is what you shall offer on the altar: two one year old lambs each day, continuously.

39 "The one lamb you shall offer in the morning and the other lamb you shall offer at twilight ;

40   and there *shall be* one-tenth *of an ephah* of fine flour mixed with one-fourth of a hin of beaten oil, and one-fourth of a hin of wine for a drink offering with one lamb.

41   "The other lamb you shall offer at twilight, and shall offer with it the same grain offering and the same drink offering as in the morning, for a soothing aroma, an offering by fire to the Lord.

42   "It shall be a continual burnt offering throughout your generations at the doorway of the tent of meeting before the Lord, where I will meet with you, to speak to you there.

43   "I will meet there with the sons of Israel, and it shall be consecrated by My glory.

44   "I will consecrate the tent of meeting and the altar; I will also consecrate Aaron and his sons to minister as priests to Me.

45   "I will dwell among the sons of Israel and will be their God.

46   "They shall know that I am the Lord their God who brought them out of the land of Egypt, that I might dwell among them; I am the Lord their God.

© *2008 Precept Ministries International*

EXODUS 30
Observation Worksheet

Chapter Theme _____

"MOREOVER, you shall make an altar as a place for burning incense; you shall make it of acacia wood.

2   "Its length *shall be* a cubit, and its width a cubit, it shall be square, and its height *shall be* two cubits; its horns *shall be* of one piece with it.

3   "You shall overlay it with pure gold, its top and its sides all around, and its horns; and you shall make a gold molding all around for it.

4   "You shall make two gold rings for it under its molding; you shall make *them* on its two side walls—on opposite sides—and they shall be holders for poles with which to carry it.

5   "You shall make the poles of acacia wood and overlay them with gold.

6   "You shall put this altar in front of the veil that is near the ark of the testimony, in front of the mercy seat that is over *the ark of* the testimony, where I will meet with you.

7   "Aaron shall burn fragrant incense on it; he shall burn it every morning when he trims the lamps.

8   "When Aaron trims the lamps at twilight, he shall burn incense. *There shall be* perpetual incense before the LORD throughout your generations.

9   "You shall not offer any strange incense on this altar, or burnt offering or meal offering; and you shall not pour out a drink offering on it.

10   "Aaron shall make atonement on its horns once a year; he shall make atonement on it with the blood of the sin offering of atonement once a year throughout your generations. It is most holy to the LORD."

11   The LORD also spoke to Moses, saying,

12   "When you take a census of the sons of Israel to number them, then each one of them shall give a ransom for himself to the LORD, when you number them, so that there will be no plague among them when you number them.

13   "This is what everyone who is numbered shall give: half a shekel according to the shekel of the sanctuary (the shekel is twenty gerahs), half a shekel as a con-

© *2008 Precept Ministries International*

tribution to the LORD.

14 "Everyone who is numbered, from twenty years old and over, shall give the contribution to the LORD.

15 "The rich shall not pay more and the poor shall not pay less than the half shekel, when you give the contribution to the LORD to make atonement for yourselves.

16 "You shall take the atonement money from the sons of Israel and shall give it for the service of the tent of meeting, that it may be a memorial for the sons of Israel before the LORD, to make atonement for yourselves."

17 The LORD spoke to Moses, saying,

18 "You shall also make a laver of bronze, with its base of bronze, for washing; and you shall put it between the tent of meeting and the altar, and you shall put water in it.

19 "Aaron and his sons shall wash their hands and their feet from it;

20 when they enter the tent of meeting, they shall wash with water, so that they will not die; or when they approach the altar to minister, by offering up in smoke a fire *sacrifice* to the LORD.

21 "So they shall wash their hands and their feet, so that they will not die; and it shall be a perpetual statute for them, for Aaron and his descendants throughout their generations."

22 Moreover, the LORD spoke to Moses, saying,

23 "Take also for yourself the finest of spices: of flowing myrrh five hundred *shekels,* and of fragrant cinnamon half as much, two hundred and fifty, and of fragrant cane two hundred and fifty,

24 and of cassia five hundred, according to the shekel of the sanctuary, and of olive oil a hin.

25 "You shall make of these a holy anointing oil, a perfume mixture, the work of a perfumer; it shall be a holy anointing oil.

26 "With it you shall anoint the tent of meeting and the ark of the testimony,

27 and the table and all its utensils, and the lampstand and its utensils, and the altar of incense,

       © *2008 Precept Ministries International*

28   and the altar of burnt offering and all its utensils, and the laver and its stand.

29   "You shall also consecrate them, that they may be most holy; whatever touches them shall be holy.

30   "You shall anoint Aaron and his sons, and consecrate them, that they may minister as priests to Me.

31   "You shall speak to the sons of Israel, saying, 'This shall be a holy anointing oil to Me throughout your generations.

32   'It shall not be poured on anyone 's body, nor shall you make *any* like it in the same proportions; it is holy, *and* it shall be holy to you.

33   'Whoever shall mix *any* like it or whoever puts any of it on a layman shall be cut off from his people.' "

34   Then the Lord said to Moses, "Take for yourself spices, stacte and onycha and galbanum, spices with pure frankincense; there shall be an equal part of each.

35   "With it you shall make incense, a perfume, the work of a perfumer, salted, pure, *and* holy.

36   "You shall beat some of it very fine, and put part of it before the testimony in the tent of meeting where I will meet with you; it shall be most holy to you.

37   "The incense which you shall make, you shall not make in the same proportions for yourselves; it shall be holy to you for the Lord.

38   "Whoever shall make *any* like it, to use as perfume, shall be cut off from his people."

© *2008 Precept Ministries International*

© *2008 Precept Ministries International*

EXODUS 31
Observation Worksheet

Chapter Theme _____

NOW the LORD spoke to Moses, saying,

2   "See, I have called by name Bezalel, the son of Uri, the son of Hur, of the tribe of Judah.

3   "I have filled him with the Spirit of God in wisdom, in understanding, in knowledge, and in all *kinds of* craftsmanship,

4   to make artistic designs for work in gold, in silver, and in bronze,

5   and in the cutting of stones for settings, and in the carving of wood, that he may work in all *kinds of* craftsmanship.

6   "And behold, I Myself have appointed with him Oholiab, the son of Ahisamach, of the tribe of Dan; and in the hearts of all who are skillful I have put skill, that they may make all that I have commanded you:

7   the tent of meeting, and the ark of testimony, and the mercy seat upon it, and all the furniture of the tent,

8   the table also and its utensils, and the pure *gold* lampstand with all its utensils, and the altar of incense,

9   the altar of burnt offering also with all its utensils, and the laver and its stand,

10   the woven garments as well, and the holy garments for Aaron the priest, and the garments of his sons, *with which* to carry on their priesthood;

11   the anointing oil also, and the fragrant incense for the holy place, they are to make *them* according to all that I have commanded you."

12   The LORD spoke to Moses, saying,

13   "But as for you, speak to the sons of Israel, saying, 'You shall surely observe My sabbaths; for *this* is a sign between Me and you throughout your generations, that you may know that I am the LORD who sanctifies you.

14   'Therefore you are to observe the sabbath, for it is holy to you. Everyone who profanes it shall surely be put to death; for whoever does any work on it, that person shall be cut off from among his people.

15   'For six days work may be done, but on the seventh day there is a sabbath of

complete rest, holy to the LORD; whoever does any work on the sabbath day shall surely be put to death.

16 'So the sons of Israel shall observe the sabbath, to celebrate the sabbath throughout their generations as a perpetual covenant.'

17 "It is a sign between Me and the sons of Israel forever; for in six days the LORD made heaven and earth, but on the seventh day He ceased *from labor,* and was refreshed."

18 When He had finished speaking with him upon Mount Sinai, He gave Moses the two tablets of the testimony, tablets of stone, written by the finger of God.

© *2008 Precept Ministries International*

EXODUS 32
Observation Worksheet

Chapter Theme _____

NOW when the people saw that Moses delayed to come down from the mountain, the people assembled about Aaron and said to him, "Come, make us a god who will go before us; as for this Moses, the man who brought us up from the land of Egypt, we do not know what has become of him."

2   Aaron said to them, "Tear off the gold rings which are in the ears of your wives, your sons, and your daughters, and bring *them* to me."

3   Then all the people tore off the gold rings which were in their ears and brought *them* to Aaron.

4   He took *this* from their hand, and fashioned it with a graving tool and made it into a molten calf; and they said, "This is your god, O Israel, who brought you up from the land of Egypt."

5   Now when Aaron saw *this,* he built an altar before it; and Aaron made a proclamation and said, "Tomorrow *shall be* a feast to the LORD."

6   So the next day they rose early and offered burnt offerings, and brought peace offerings; and the people sat down to eat and to drink, and rose up to play.

7   Then the LORD spoke to Moses, "Go down at once, for your people, whom you brought up from the land of Egypt, have corrupted *themselves.*

8   "They have quickly turned aside from the way which I commanded them. They have made for themselves a molten calf, and have worshiped it and have sacrificed to it and said, 'This is your god, O Israel, who brought you up from the land of Egypt!' "

9   The LORD said to Moses, "I have seen this people, and behold, they are an obstinate people.

10   "Now then let Me alone, that My anger may burn against them and that I may destroy them; and I will make of you a great nation."

11   Then Moses entreated the LORD his God, and said, "O LORD, why does Your anger burn against Your people whom You have brought out from the land of Egypt with great power and with a mighty hand?

12   "Why should the Egyptians speak, saying, 'With evil intent He brought them out

to kill them in the mountains and to destroy them from the face of the earth'? Turn from Your burning anger and change Your mind about doing harm to Your people.

13   "Remember Abraham, Isaac, and Israel, Your servants to whom You swore by Yourself, and said to them, 'I will multiply your descendants as the stars of the heavens, and all this land of which I have spoken I will give to your descendants, and they shall inherit it forever.' "

14   So the Lord changed His mind about the harm which He said He would do to His people.

15   Then Moses turned and went down from the mountain with the two tablets of the testimony in his hand, tablets which were written on both sides ; they were written on one side and the other.

16   The tablets were God's work, and the writing was God's writing engraved on the tablets.

17   Now when Joshua heard the sound of the people as they shouted, he said to Moses, "There is a sound of war in the camp."

18   But he said, "It is not the sound of the cry of triumph, Nor is it the sound of the cry of defeat; But the sound of singing I hear."

19   It came about, as soon as Moses came near the camp, that he saw the calf and the dancing; and Moses' anger burned, and he threw the tablets from his hands and shattered them at the foot of the mountain.

20   He took the calf which they had made and burned it with fire, and ground it to powder, and scattered it over the surface of the water and made the sons of Israel drink it.

21   Then Moses said to Aaron, "What did this people do to you, that you have brought such great sin upon them?"

22   Aaron said, "Do not let the anger of my lord burn; you know the people yourself, that they are prone to evil.

23   "For they said to me, 'Make a god for us who will go before us; for this Moses,

 © *2008 Precept Ministries International*

the man who brought us up from the land of Egypt, we do not know what has become of him.'

24 "I said to them, 'Whoever has any gold, let them tear it off.' So they gave it to me, and I threw it into the fire, and out came this calf."

25 Now when Moses saw that the people were out of control—for Aaron had let them get out of control to be a derision among their enemies—

26 then Moses stood in the gate of the camp, and said, "Whoever is for the LORD, come to me!" And all the sons of Levi gathered together to him.

27 He said to them, "Thus says the LORD, the God of Israel, 'Every man of you put his sword upon his thigh, and go back and forth from gate to gate in the camp, and kill every man his brother, and every man his friend, and every man his neighbor.' "

28 So the sons of Levi did as Moses instructed, and about three thousand men of the people fell that day.

29 Then Moses said, "Dedicate yourselves today to the LORD—for every man has been against his son and against his brother—in order that He may bestow a blessing upon you today."

30 On the next day Moses said to the people, "You yourselves have committed a great sin; and now I am going up to the LORD, perhaps I can make atonement for your sin."

31 Then Moses returned to the LORD, and said, "Alas, this people has committed a great sin, and they have made a god of gold for themselves.

32 "But now, if You will, forgive their sin—and if not, please blot me out from Your book which You have written!"

33 The LORD said to Moses, "Whoever has sinned against Me, I will blot him out of My book.

34 "But go now, lead the people where I told you. Behold, My angel shall go before you; nevertheless in the day when I punish, I will punish them for their sin."

35 Then the LORD smote the people, because of what they did with the calf which Aaron had made.

© *2008 Precept Ministries International*

EXODUS 33
Observation Worksheet

Chapter Theme _____

THEN the LORD spoke to Moses, "Depart, go up from here, you and the people whom you have brought up from the land of Egypt, to the land of which I swore to Abraham, Isaac, and Jacob, saying, 'To your descendants I will give it.'

2   "I will send an angel before you and I will drive out the Canaanite, the Amorite, the Hittite, the Perizzite, the Hivite and the Jebusite.

3   "*Go up* to a land flowing with milk and honey; for I will not go up in your midst, because you are an obstinate people, and I might destroy you on the way."

4   When the people heard this sad word, they went into mourning, and none of them put on his ornaments.

5   For the LORD had said to Moses, "Say to the sons of Israel, 'You are an obstinate people; should I go up in your midst for one moment, I would destroy you. Now therefore, put off your ornaments from you, that I may know what I shall do with you.' "

6   So the sons of Israel stripped themselves of their ornaments, from Mount Horeb *onward.*

7   Now Moses used to take the tent and pitch it outside the camp, a good distance from the camp, and he called it the tent of meeting. And everyone who sought the LORD would go out to the tent of meeting which was outside the camp.

8   And it came about, whenever Moses went out to the tent, that all the people would arise and stand, each at the entrance of his tent, and gaze after Moses until he entered the tent.

9   Whenever Moses entered the tent, the pillar of cloud would descend and stand at the entrance of the tent; and the LORD would speak with Moses.

10 When all the people saw the pillar of cloud standing at the entrance of the tent, all the people would arise and worship, each at the entrance of his tent.

11 Thus the LORD used to speak to Moses face to face, just as a man speaks to his friend. When Moses returned to the camp, his servant Joshua, the son of Nun, a young man, would not depart from the tent.

12 Then Moses said to the LORD, "See, You say to me, 'Bring up this people!' But

You Yourself have not let me know whom You will send with me. Moreover, You have said, 'I have known you by name, and you have also found favor in My sight.'

13 "Now therefore, I pray You, if I have found favor in Your sight, let me know Your ways that I may know You, so that I may find favor in Your sight. Consider too, that this nation is Your people."

14 And He said, "My presence shall go *with you,* and I will give you rest."

15 Then he said to Him, "If Your presence does not go *with us,* do not lead us up from here.

16 "For how then can it be known that I have found favor in Your sight, I and Your people? Is it not by Your going with us, so that we, I and Your people, may be distinguished from all the *other* people who are upon the face of the earth ?"

17 The LORD said to Moses, "I will also do this thing of which you have spoken; for you have found favor in My sight and I have known you by name."

18 Then Moses said, "I pray You, show me Your glory!"

19 And He said, "I Myself will make all My goodness pass before you, and will proclaim the name of the LORD before you; and I will be gracious to whom I will be gracious, and will show compassion on whom I will show compassion."

20 But He said, "You cannot see My face, for no man can see Me and live!"

21 Then the LORD said, "Behold, there is a place by Me, and you shall stand *there* on the rock;

22 and it will come about, while My glory is passing by, that I will put you in the cleft of the rock and cover you with My hand until I have passed by.

23 "Then I will take My hand away and you shall see My back, but My face shall not be seen."

© 2008 Precept Ministries International

EXODUS 34
Observation Worksheet

Chapter Theme _____

NOW the LORD said to Moses, "Cut out for yourself two stone tablets like the former ones, and I will write on the tablets the words that were on the former tablets which you shattered.

2 "So be ready by morning, and come up in the morning to Mount Sinai, and present yourself there to Me on the top of the mountain.

3 "No man is to come up with you, nor let any man be seen anywhere on the mountain; even the flocks and the herds may not graze in front of that mountain."

4 So he cut out two stone tablets like the former ones, and Moses rose up early in the morning and went up to Mount Sinai, as the LORD had commanded him, and he took two stone tablets in his hand.

5 The LORD descended in the cloud and stood there with him as he called upon the name of the LORD.

6 Then the LORD passed by in front of him and proclaimed, "The LORD, the LORD God, compassionate and gracious, slow to anger, and abounding in lovingkindness and truth ;

7 who keeps lovingkindness for thousands, who forgives iniquity, transgression and sin; yet He will by no means leave *the guilty* unpunished, visiting the iniquity of fathers on the children and on the grandchildren to the third and fourth generations."

8 Moses made haste to bow low toward the earth and worship.

9 He said, "If now I have found favor in Your sight, O Lord, I pray, let the Lord go along in our midst, even though the people are so obstinate, and pardon our iniquity and our sin, and take us as Your own possession."

10 Then God said, "Behold, I am going to make a covenant. Before all your people I will perform miracles which have not been produced in all the earth nor among any of the nations; and all the people among whom you live will see the working of the LORD, for it is a fearful thing that I am going to perform with you.

11 "Be sure to observe what I am commanding you this day: behold, I am going to

© 2008 Precept Ministries International

drive out the Amorite before you, and the Canaanite, the Hittite, the Perizzite, the Hivite and the Jebusite.

12   "Watch yourself that you make no covenant with the inhabitants of the land into which you are going, or it will become a snare in your midst.

13   "But *rather,* you are to tear down their altars and smash their *sacred* pillars and cut down their Asherim

14   —for you shall not worship any other god, for the L ORD, whose name is Jealous, is a jealous God—

15   otherwise you might make a covenant with the inhabitants of the land and they would play the harlot with their gods and sacrifice to their gods, and someone might invite you to eat of his sacrifice,

16   and you might take some of his daughters for your sons, and his daughters might play the harlot with their gods and cause your sons *also* to play the harlot with their gods.

17   "You shall make for yourself no molten gods.

18   "You shall observe the Feast of Unleavened Bread. For seven days you are to eat unleavened bread, as I commanded you, at the appointed time in the month of Abib, for in the month of Abib you came out of Egypt.

19   "The first offspring from every womb belongs to Me, and all your male livestock, the first offspring from cattle and sheep.

20   "You shall redeem with a lamb the first offspring from a donkey; and if you do not redeem *it,* then you shall break its neck. You shall redeem all the firstborn of your sons. None shall appear before Me empty-handed.

21   "You shall work six days, but on the seventh day you shall rest; *even* during plowing time and harvest you shall rest.

22   "You shall celebrate the Feast of Weeks, *that is,* the first fruits of the wheat harvest, and the Feast of Ingathering at the turn of the year.

    © 2008 Precept Ministries International

23 "Three times a year all your males are to appear before the Lord GOD, the God of Israel.

24 "For I will drive out nations before you and enlarge your borders, and no man shall covet your land when you go up three times a year to appear before the LORD your God.

25 "You shall not offer the blood of My sacrifice with leavened bread, nor is the sacrifice of the Feast of the Passover to be left over until morning.

26 "You shall bring the very first of the first fruits of your soil into the house of the LORD your God. "You shall not boil a young goat in its mother's milk."

27 Then the LORD said to Moses, "Write down these words, for in accordance with these words I have made a covenant with you and with Israel."

28 So he was there with the LORD forty days and forty nights; he did not eat bread or drink water. And he wrote on the tablets the words of the covenant, the Ten Commandments.

29 It came about when Moses was coming down from Mount Sinai (and the two tablets of the testimony *were* in Moses' hand as he was coming down from the mountain), that Moses did not know that the skin of his face shone because of his speaking with Him.

30 So when Aaron and all the sons of Israel saw Moses, behold, the skin of his face shone, and they were afraid to come near him.

31 Then Moses called to them, and Aaron and all the rulers in the congregation returned to him; and Moses spoke to them.

32 Afterward all the sons of Israel came near, and he commanded them *to do* everything that the LORD had spoken to him on Mount Sinai.

33 When Moses had finished speaking with them, he put a veil over his face.

34 But whenever Moses went in before the LORD to speak with Him, he would take off the veil until he came out; and whenever he came out and spoke to the sons of Israel what he had been commanded,

35   the sons of Israel would see the face of Moses, that the skin of Moses' face

       shone. So Moses would replace the veil over his face until he went in to speak

       with Him.

                                            © *2008 Precept Ministries International*

EXODUS 35
Observation Worksheet

Chapter Theme _____

THEN Moses assembled all the congregation of the sons of Israel, and said to them, "These are the things that the LORD has commanded *you* to do :

2   "For six days work may be done, but on the seventh day you shall have a holy *day,* a sabbath of complete rest to the LORD; whoever does any work on it shall be put to death.

3   "You shall not kindle a fire in any of your dwellings on the sabbath day."

4   Moses spoke to all the congregation of the sons of Israel, saying, "This is the thing which the LORD has commanded, saying,"

5   'Take from among you a contribution to the LORD; whoever is of a willing heart, let him bring it as the LORD'S contribution : gold, silver, and bronze,

6   and blue, purple and scarlet *material,* fine linen, goats' *hair,*

7   and rams' skins dyed red, and porpoise skins, and acacia wood,

8   and oil for lighting, and spices for the anointing oil, and for the fragrant incense,

9   and onyx stones and setting stones for the ephod and for the breastpiece

10 'Let every skillful man among you come, and make all that the LORD has commanded:

11 the tabernacle, its tent and its covering, its hooks and its boards, its bars, its pillars, and its sockets;

12 the ark and its poles, the mercy seat, and the curtain of the screen;

13 the table and its poles, and all its utensils, and the bread of the Presence;

14 the lampstand also for the light and its utensils and its lamps and the oil for the light;

15 and the altar of incense and its poles, and the anointing oil and the fragrant incense, and the screen for the doorway at the entrance of the tabernacle;

16 the altar of burnt offering with its bronze grating, its poles, and all its utensils,

© 2008 Precept Ministries International

the basin and its stand;

17   the hangings of the court, its pillars and its sockets, and the screen for the gate of the court;

18   the pegs of the tabernacle and the pegs of the court and their cords;

19   the woven garments for ministering in the holy place, the holy garments for Aaron the priest and the garments of his sons, to minister as priests.'"

20   Then all the congregation of the sons of Israel departed from Moses' presence.

21   Everyone whose heart stirred him and everyone whose spirit moved him came *and* brought the Lord'S contribution for the work of the tent of meeting and for all its service and for the holy garments.

22   Then all whose hearts moved them, both men and women, came *and* brought brooches and earrings and signet rings and bracelets, all articles of gold; so *did* every man who presented an offering of gold to the Lord.

23   Every man, who had in his possession blue and purple and scarlet *material* and fine linen and goats' *hair* and rams' skins dyed red and porpoise skins, brought them.

24   Everyone who could make a contribution of silver and bronze brought the Lord'S contribution ; and every man who had in his possession acacia wood for any work of the service brought it.

25   All the skilled women spun with their hands, and brought what they had spun, *in* blue and purple *and* scarlet *material* and *in* fine linen.

26   All the women whose heart stirred with a skill spun the goats' *hair.*

27   The rulers brought the onyx stones and the stones for setting for the ephod and for the breastpiece ;

28   and the spice and the oil for the light and for the anointing oil and for the fragrant incense.

29   The Israelites, all the men and women, whose heart moved them to bring *material* for all the work, which the Lord had commanded through Moses to be done, brought a freewill offering to the Lord.

30   Then Moses said to the sons of Israel, "See, the Lord has called by name Beza-

© *2008 Precept Ministries International*

lel the son of Uri, the son of Hur, of the tribe of Judah.

31 "And He has filled him with the Spirit of God, in wisdom, in understanding and in knowledge and in all craftsmanship ;

32 to make designs for working in gold and in silver and in bronze,

33 and in the cutting of stones for settings and in the carving of wood, so as to perform in every inventive work.

34 "He also has put in his heart to teach, both he and Oholiab, the son of Ahisamach, of the tribe of Dan.

35 "He has filled them with skill to perform every work of an engraver and of a designer and of an embroiderer, in blue and in purple *and* in scarlet *material,* and in fine linen, and of a weaver, as performers of every work and makers of designs.

© *2008 Precept Ministries International*

© *2008 Precept Ministries International*

EXODUS 36
Observation Worksheet

Chapter Theme _____

"NOW Bezalel and Oholiab, and every skillful person in whom the LORD has put skill and understanding to know how to perform all the work in the construction of the sanctuary, shall perform in accordance with all that the LORD has commanded."

2 Then Moses called Bezalel and Oholiab and every skillful person in whom the LORD had put skill, everyone whose heart stirred him, to come to the work to perform it.

3 They received from Moses all the contributions which the sons of Israel had brought to perform the work in the construction of the sanctuary. And they still *continued* bringing to him freewill offerings every morning.

4 And all the skillful men who were performing all the work of the sanctuary came, each from the work which he was performing,

5 and they said to Moses, "The people are bringing much more than enough for the construction work which the LORD commanded *us* to perform."

6 So Moses issued a command, and a proclamation was circulated throughout the camp, saying, "Let no man or woman any longer perform work for the contributions of the sanctuary." Thus the people were restrained from bringing *any more.*

7 For the material they had was sufficient and more than enough for all the work, to perform it.

8 All the skillful men among those who were performing the work made the tabernacle with ten curtains; of fine twisted linen and blue and purple and scarlet *material,* with cherubim, the work of a skillful workman, Bezalel made them.

9 The length of each curtain was twenty-eight cubits and the width of each curtain four cubits ; all the curtains had the same measurements.

10 He joined five curtains to one another and *the other* five curtains he joined to one another.

11 He made loops of blue on the edge of the outermost curtain in the first set ; he did likewise on the edge of the curtain that was outermost in the second set.

© 2008 Precept Ministries International

12   He made fifty loops in the one curtain and he made fifty loops on the edge of the curtain that was in the second set ; the loops were opposite each other.

13   He made fifty clasps of gold and joined the curtains to one another with the clasps, so the tabernacle was a unit.

14   Then he made curtains of goats' *hair* for a tent over the tabernacle; he made eleven curtains in all.

15   The length of each curtain *was* thirty cubits and four cubits the width of each curtain; the eleven curtains had the same measurements.

16   He joined five curtains by themselves and *the other* six curtains by themselves.

17   Moreover, he made fifty loops on the edge of the curtain that was outermost in the *first* set, and he made fifty loops on the edge of the curtain *that was outermost in* the second set.

18   He made fifty clasps of bronze to join the tent together so that it would be a unit.

19   He made a covering for the tent of rams' skins dyed red, and a covering of porpoise skins above.

20   Then he made the boards for the tabernacle of acacia wood, standing upright.

21   Ten cubits *was* the length of each board and one and a half cubits the width of each board.

22   *There were* two tenons for each board, fitted to one another; thus he did for all the boards of the tabernacle.

23   He made the boards for the tabernacle: twenty boards for the south side;

24   and he made forty sockets of silver under the twenty boards; two sockets under one board for its two tenons and two sockets under another board for its two tenons.

25   Then for the second side of the tabernacle, on the north side, he made twenty boards,

26   and their forty sockets of silver; two sockets under one board and two sockets under another board.

27   For the rear of the tabernacle, to the west, he made six boards.

                                    © *2008 Precept Ministries International*

28 He made two boards for the corners of the tabernacle at the rear.

29 They were double beneath, and together they were complete to its top to the first ring; thus he did with both of them for the two corners.

30 There were eight boards with their sockets of silver, sixteen sockets, two under every board.

31 Then he made bars of acacia wood, five for the boards of one side of the tabernacle,

32 and five bars for the boards of the other side of the tabernacle, and five bars for the boards of the tabernacle for the rear *side* to the west.

33 He made the middle bar to pass through in the center of the boards from end to end.

34 He overlaid the boards with gold and made their rings of gold *as* holders for the bars, and overlaid the bars with gold.

35 Moreover, he made the veil of blue and purple and scarlet *material,* and fine twisted linen; he made it with cherubim, the work of a skillful workman.

36 He made four pillars of acacia for it, and overlaid them with gold, with their hooks of gold; and he cast four sockets of silver for them.

37 He made a screen for the doorway of the tent, of blue and purple and scarlet *material,* and fine twisted linen, the work of a weaver ;

38 and *he made* its five pillars with their hooks, and he overlaid their tops and their bands with gold; but their five sockets were of bronze.

© 2008 Precept Ministries International

© *2008 Precept Ministries International*

EXODUS 37
Observation Worksheet

Chapter Theme _____

NOW Bezalel made the ark of acacia wood; its length was two and a half cubits, and its width one and a half cubits, and its height one and a half cubits;

2   and he overlaid it with pure gold inside and out, and made a gold molding for it all around.

3   He cast four rings of gold for it on its four feet; even two rings on one side of it, and two rings on the other side of it.

4   He made poles of acacia wood and overlaid them with gold.

5   He put the poles into the rings on the sides of the ark, to carry it.

6   He made a mercy seat of pure gold, two and a half cubits long and one and a half cubits wide.

7   He made two cherubim of gold; he made them of hammered work at the two ends of the mercy seat;

8   one cherub at the one end and one cherub at the other end; he made the cherubim *of one piece* with the mercy seat at the two ends.

9   The cherubim had *their* wings spread upward, covering the mercy seat with their wings, with their faces toward each other; the faces of the cherubim were toward the mercy seat.

10   Then he made the table of acacia wood, two cubits long and a cubit wide and one and a half cubits high.

11   He overlaid it with pure gold, and made a gold molding for it all around.

12   He made a rim for it of a handbreadth all around, and made a gold molding for its rim all around.

13   He cast four gold rings for it and put the rings on the four corners that were on its four feet.

14   Close by the rim were the rings, the holders for the poles to carry the table.

15   He made the poles of acacia wood and overlaid them with gold, to carry the table.

© *2008 Precept Ministries International*

16 He made the utensils which were on the table, its dishes and its pans and its bowls and its jars, with which to pour out drink offerings, of pure gold.

17 Then he made the lampstand of pure gold. He made the lampstand of hammered work, its base and its shaft; its cups, its bulbs and its flowers were *of one piece* with it.

18 There were six branches going out of its sides; three branches of the lampstand from the one side of it and three branches of the lampstand from the other side of it;

19 three cups shaped like almond *blossoms,* a bulb and a flower in one branch, and three cups shaped like almond *blossoms,* a bulb and a flower in the other branch—so for the six branches going out of the lampstand.

20 In the lampstand *there were* four cups shaped like almond *blossoms,* its bulbs and its flowers;

21 and a bulb was under the *first* pair of branches *coming* out of it, and a bulb under the *second* pair of branches *coming* out of it, and a bulb under the *third* pair of branches *coming* out of it, for the six branches coming out of the lampstand.

22 Their bulbs and their branches were *of one piece* with it; the whole of it *was* a single hammered work of pure gold.

23 He made its seven lamps with its snuffers and its trays of pure gold.

24 He made it and all its utensils from a talent of pure gold.

25 Then he made the altar of incense of acacia wood: a cubit long and a cubit wide, square, and two cubits high ; its horns were *of one piece* with it.

26 He overlaid it with pure gold, its top and its sides all around, and its horns; and he made a gold molding for it all around.

27 He made two golden rings for it under its molding, on its two sides—on opposite sides—as holders for poles with which to carry it.

28 He made the poles of acacia wood and overlaid them with gold.

29 And he made the holy anointing oil and the pure, fragrant incense of spices, the work of a perfumer.

          © *2008 Precept Ministries International*

EXODUS 38
Observation Worksheet

Chapter Theme _____

THEN he made the altar of burnt offering of acacia wood, five cubits long, and five cubits wide, square, and three cubits high.

2   He made its horns on its four corners, its horns being *of one piece* with it, and he overlaid it with bronze.

3   He made all the utensils of the altar, the pails and the shovels and the basins, the flesh hooks and the firepans; he made all its utensils of bronze.

4   He made for the altar a grating of bronze network beneath, under its ledge, reaching halfway up.

5   He cast four rings on the four ends of the bronze grating *as* holders for the poles.

6   He made the poles of acacia wood and overlaid them with bronze.

7   He inserted the poles into the rings on the sides of the altar, with which to carry it. He made it hollow with planks.

8   Moreover, he made the laver of bronze with its base of bronze, from the mirrors of the serving women who served at the doorway of the tent of meeting.

9   Then he made the court: for the south side the hangings of the court were of fine twisted linen, one hundred cubits;

10   their twenty pillars, and their twenty sockets, *made* of bronze; the hooks of the pillars and their bands *were* of silver.

11   For the north side *there were* one hundred cubits; their twenty pillars and their twenty sockets *were* of bronze, the hooks of the pillars and their bands *were* of silver.

12   For the west side *there were* hangings of fifty cubits *with* their ten pillars and their ten sockets ; the hooks of the pillars and their bands *were* of silver.

13   For the east side fifty cubits.

14   The hangings for the *one* side *of the gate were* fifteen cubits, *with* their three pillars and their three sockets,

15   and so for the other side. On both sides of the gate of the court *were* hangings of fifteen cubits, *with* their three pillars and their three sockets.

© 2008 Precept Ministries International

16   All the hangings of the court all around *were* of fine twisted linen.

17   The sockets for the pillars *were* of bronze, the hooks of the pillars and their bands, of silver; and the overlaying of their tops, of silver, and all the pillars of the court were furnished with silver bands.

18   The screen of the gate of the court was the work of the weaver, of blue and purple and scarlet *material* and fine twisted linen. And the length *was* twenty cubits and the height *was* five cubits, corresponding to the hangings of the court.

19   Their four pillars and their four sockets *were* of bronze; their hooks *were* of silver, and the overlaying of their tops and their bands *were* of silver.

20   All the pegs of the tabernacle and of the court all around *were* of bronze.

21   This is the number of the things for the tabernacle, the tabernacle of the testimony, as they were numbered according to the command of Moses, for the service of the Levites, by the hand of Ithamar the son of Aaron the priest.

22   Now Bezalel the son of Uri, the son of Hur, of the tribe of Judah, made all that the LORD had commanded Moses.

23   With him *was* Oholiab the son of Ahisamach, of the tribe of Dan, an engraver and a skillful workman and a weaver in blue and in purple and in scarlet *material,* and fine linen.

24   All the gold that was used for the work, in all the work of the sanctuary, even the gold of the wave offering, was 29 talents and 730 shekels, according to the shekel of the sanctuary.

25   The silver of those of the congregation who were numbered was 100 talents and 1,775 shekels, according to the shekel of the sanctuary;

26   a beka a head (*that is,* half a shekel according to the shekel of the sanctuary), for each one who passed over to those who were numbered, from twenty years old and upward, for 603,550 men.

27   The hundred talents of silver were for casting the sockets of the sanctuary and the sockets of the veil; one hundred sockets for the hundred talents, a talent for a socket.

© *2008 Precept Ministries International*

28   Of the 1,775 *shekels,* he made hooks for the pillars and overlaid their tops and made bands for them.

29   The bronze of the wave offering was 70 talents and 2,400 shekels.

30   With it he made the sockets to the doorway of the tent of meeting, and the bronze altar and its bronze grating, and all the utensils of the altar,

31   and the sockets of the court all around and the sockets of the gate of the court, and all the pegs of the tabernacle and all the pegs of the court all around.

© *2008 Precept Ministries International*

Exodus

Exodus 38

© 2008 Precept Ministries International

EXODUS 39
Observation Worksheet

Chapter Theme _____

MOREOVER, from the blue and purple and scarlet *material,* they made finely woven garments for ministering in the holy place as well as the holy garments which were for Aaron, just as the LORD had commanded Moses.

2   He made the ephod of gold, *and* of blue and purple and scarlet *material,* and fine twisted linen.

3   Then they hammered out gold sheets and cut *them* into threads to be woven in *with* the blue and the purple and the scarlet *material,* and the fine linen, the work of a skillful workman.

4   They made attaching shoulder pieces for the ephod; it was attached at its two *upper* ends.

5   The skillfully woven band which was on it was like its workmanship, of the same material: of gold *and* of blue and purple and scarlet *material,* and fine twisted linen, just as the LORD had commanded Moses.

6   They made the onyx stones, set in gold filigree *settings;* they were engraved *like* the engravings of a signet, according to the names of the sons of Israel.

7   And he placed them on the shoulder pieces of the ephod, *as* memorial stones for the sons of Israel, just as the LORD had commanded Moses.

8   He made the breastpiece, the work of a skillful workman, like the workmanship of the ephod: of gold *and* of blue and purple and scarlet *material* and fine twisted linen.

9   It was square; they made the breastpiece folded double, a span long and a span wide when folded double.

10   And they mounted four rows of stones on it. The first row *was* a row of ruby, topaz, and emerald;

11   and the second row, a turquoise, a sapphire and a diamond;

12   and the third row, a jacinth, an agate, and an amethyst;

13   and the fourth row, a beryl, an onyx, and a jasper. They were set in gold filigree *settings* when they were mounted.

14   The stones were corresponding to the names of the sons of Israel; they were twelve, corresponding to their names, *engraved with* the engravings of a signet, each with its name for the twelve tribes.

15   They made on the breastpiece chains like cords, of twisted cordage work in pure gold.

16   They made two gold filigree *settings* and two gold rings, and put the two rings on the two ends of the breastpiece.

17   Then they put the two gold cords in the two rings at the ends of the breastpiece.

18   They put the *other* two ends of the two cords on the two filigree *settings,* and put them on the shoulder pieces of the ephod at the front of it.

19   They made two gold rings and placed *them* on the two ends of the breastpiece, on its inner edge which was next to the ephod.

20   Furthermore, they made two gold rings and placed them on the bottom of the two shoulder pieces of the ephod, on the front of it, close to the place where it joined, above the woven band of the ephod.

21   They bound the breastpiece by its rings to the rings of the ephod with a blue cord, so that it would be on the woven band of the ephod, and that the breastpiece would not come loose from the ephod, just as the LORD had commanded Moses.

22   Then he made the robe of the ephod of woven work, all of blue ;

23   and the opening of the robe was *at the top* in the center, as the opening of a coat of mail, with a binding all around its opening, so that it would not be torn.

24   They made pomegranates of blue and purple and scarlet *material and* twisted *linen* on the hem of the robe.

25   They also made bells of pure gold, and put the bells between the pomegranates all around on the hem of the robe,

26   alternating a bell and a pomegranate all around on the hem of the robe for the service, just as the LORD had commanded Moses.

27   They made the tunics of finely woven linen for Aaron and his sons,

© *2008 Precept Ministries International*

28 and the turban of fine linen, and the decorated caps of fine linen, and the linen breeches of fine twisted linen,

29 and the sash of fine twisted linen, and blue and purple and scarlet *material,* the work of the weaver, just as the L ORD had commanded Moses.

30 They made the plate of the holy crown of pure gold, and inscribed it like the engravings of a signet, "Holy to the L ORD."

31 They fastened a blue cord to it, to fasten it on the turban above, just as the L ORD had commanded Moses.

32 Thus all the work of the tabernacle of the tent of meeting was completed; and the sons of Israel did according to all that the L ORD had commanded Moses; so they did.

33 They brought the tabernacle to Moses, the tent and all its furnishings : its clasps, its boards, its bars, and its pillars and its sockets ;

34 and the covering of rams' skins dyed red, and the covering of porpoise skins, and the screening veil;

35 the ark of the testimony and its poles and the mercy seat;

36 the table, all its utensils, and the bread of the Presence ;

37 the pure *gold* lampstand, with its arrangement of lamps and all its utensils, and the oil for the light;

38 and the gold altar, and the anointing oil and the fragrant incense, and the veil for the doorway of the tent;

39 the bronze altar and its bronze grating, its poles and all its utensils, the laver and its stand;

40 the hangings for the court, its pillars and its sockets, and the screen for the gate of the court, its cords and its pegs and all the equipment for the service of the tabernacle, for the tent of meeting;

41 the woven garments for ministering in the holy place and the holy garments for Aaron the priest and the garments of his sons, to minister as priests.

42 So the sons of Israel did all the work according to all that the L ORD had commanded Moses.

43   And Moses examined all the work and behold, they had done it; just as the LORD

had commanded, this they had done. So Moses blessed thcm.

© *2008 Precept Ministries International*

EXODUS 40
Observation Worksheet

Chapter Theme _____

THEN the LORD spoke to Moses, saying,

2 "On the first day of the first month you shall set up the tabernacle of the tent of meeting.

3 "You shall place the ark of the testimony there, and you shall screen the ark with the veil.

4 "You shall bring in the table and arrange what belongs on it; and you shall bring in the lampstand and mount its lamps.

5 "Moreover, you shall set the gold altar of incense before the ark of the testimony, and set up the veil for the doorway to the tabernacle.

6 "You shall set the altar of burnt offering in front of the doorway of the tabernacle of the tent of meeting.

7 "You shall set the laver between the tent of meeting and the altar and put water in it.

8 "You shall set up the court all around and hang up the veil for the gateway of the court.

9 "Then you shall take the anointing oil and anoint the tabernacle and all that is in it, and shall consecrate it and all its furnishings ; and it shall be holy.

10 "You shall anoint the altar of burnt offering and all its utensils, and consecrate the altar, and the altar shall be most holy.

11 "You shall anoint the laver and its stand, and consecrate it.

12 "Then you shall bring Aaron and his sons to the doorway of the tent of meeting and wash them with water.

13 "You shall put the holy garments on Aaron and anoint him and consecrate him, that he may minister as a priest to Me.

14 "You shall bring his sons and put tunics on them;

15 and you shall anoint them even as you have anointed their father, that they may minister as priests to Me; and their anointing will qualify them for a perpetual priesthood throughout their generations."

16 Thus Moses did; according to all that the LORD had commanded him, so he did.

17 Now in the first month of the second year, on the first *day* of the month, the tabernacle was erected.

18 Moses erected the tabernacle and laid its sockets, and set up its boards, and inserted its bars and erected its pillars.

19 He spread the tent over the tabernacle and put the covering of the tent on top of it, just as the LORD had commanded Moses

20 Then he took the testimony and put *it* into the ark, and attached the poles to the ark, and put the mercy seat on top of the ark.

21 He brought the ark into the tabernacle, and set up a veil for the screen, and screened off the ark of the testimony, just as the LORD had commanded Moses.

22 Then he put the table in the tent of meeting on the north side of the tabernacle, outside the veil.

23 He set the arrangement of bread in order on it before the LORD, just as the LORD had commanded Moses.

24 Then he placed the lampstand in the tent of meeting, opposite the table, on the south side of the tabernacle.

25 He lighted the lamps before the LORD, just as the LORD had commanded Moses.

26 Then he placed the gold altar in the tent of meeting in front of the veil;

27 and he burned fragrant incense on it, just as the LORD had commanded Moses.

28 Then he set up the veil for the doorway of the tabernacle.

29 He set the altar of burnt offering *before* the doorway of the tabernacle of the tent of meeting, and offered on it the burnt offering and the meal offering, just as the LORD had commanded Moses.

30 He placed the laver between the tent of meeting and the altar and put water in it for washing.

31 From it Moses and Aaron and his sons washed their hands and their feet.

32 When they entered the tent of meeting, and when they approached the altar, they washed, just as the LORD had commanded Moses.

33 He erected the court all around the tabernacle and the altar, and hung up the veil for the gateway of the court. Thus Moses finished the work.

34 Then the cloud covered the tent of meeting, and the glory of the LORD filled the tabernacle.

35 Moses was not able to enter the tent of meeting because the cloud had settled on it, and the glory of the LORD filled the tabernacle.

36 Throughout all their journeys whenever the cloud was taken up from over the tabernacle, the sons of Israel would set out;

37 but if the cloud was not taken up, then they did not set out until the day when it was taken up.

38 For throughout all their journeys, the cloud of the LORD was on the tabernacle by day, and there was fire in it by night, in the sight of all the house of Israel.

© *2008 Precept Ministries International*

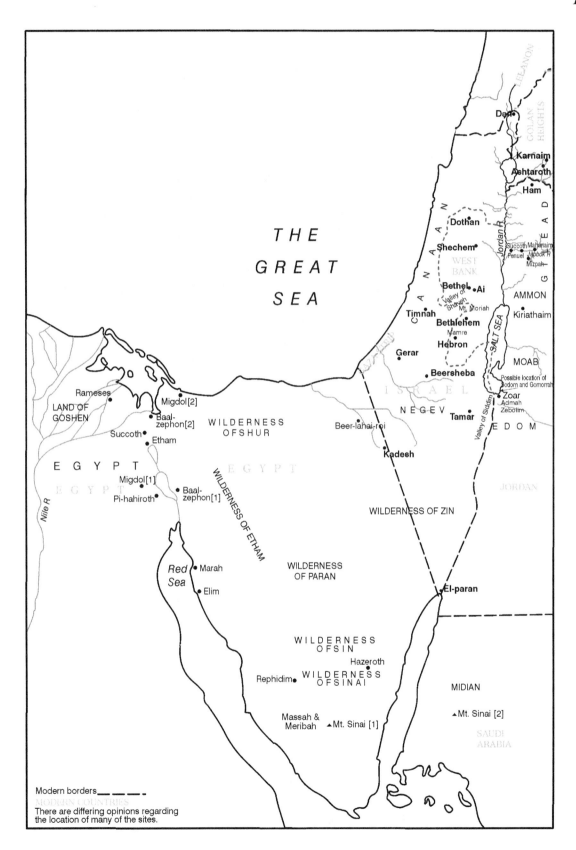

THE GREAT SEA

LEBANON

GOLAN HEIGHTS

Dan

Karnaim

Ashtaroth

Ham

C A N A A N

Dothan

Shechem

Jordan R

Succoth Mahanaim

Penuel Jabbok R

Mizpah

WEST BANK

Bethel • Ai

Valley of Shaveh

Mt. Moriah

AMMON

G I L E A D

Timnah

Bethlehem

Mamre

Hebron

Kiriathaim

SALT SEA

Gerar

MOAB

Beersheba

Possible location of Sodom and Gomorrah

I S R A E L

Zoar

Admah

Zeboiim

N E G E V

Tamar

Beer-lahai-roi

E D O M

Valley of Siddim

Rameses

LAND OF GOSHEN

Migdol[2]

Baal-zephon[2]

WILDERNESS OF SHUR

E G Y P T

Succoth

Etham

E G Y P T

Migdol[1]

Pi-hahiroth

Baal-zephon[1]

WILDERNESS OF ETHAM

Nile R

Kadesh

JORDAN

WILDERNESS OF ZIN

Red Sea

Marah

Elim

WILDERNESS OF PARAN

El-paran

WILDERNESS OF SIN

Hazeroth

Rephidim

WILDERNESS OF SINAI

MIDIAN

▲Mt. Sinai [2]

Massah & Meribah

▲Mt. Sinai [1]

SAUDI ARABIA

Modern borders _ _ _ _ _

MODERN COUNTRIES

There are differing opinions regarding the location of many of the sites.

© 2008 Precept Ministries International

AT A GLANCE CHART

BOOK THEME:

KEY
WORDS &
PHRASES:

CHAPTER
THEMES:

1	
2	
3	
4	
5	
6	
7	
8	
9	
10	
11	
12	
13	
14	
15	
16	
17	
18	
19	
20	
21	
22	
23	
24	
25	

© 2008 Precept Ministries International

AT A GLANCE CHART

BOOK THEME:

KEY
WORDS &
PHRASES:

CHAPTER
THEMES:

26	
27	
28	
29	
30	
31	
32	
33	
34	
35	
36	
37	
38	
39	
40	

Exodus

© 2008 Precept Ministries International

Exodus

© 2008 Precept Ministries International

© 2008 Precept Ministries International

MY JOURNAL ON GOD

Exodus

CPSIA information can be obtained at www.ICGtesting.com
Printed in the USA
BVOW07s2136100116

432177BV00009B/15/P